17th Workshop on Multiword Expressions (MWE 2021)

Held online due to COVID-19

Bangkok, Thailand
6 August 2021

ISBN: 978-1-7138-3381-9

MWE 2021

The 17th Workshop on Multiword Expressions

Proceedings of the Workshop

August 6, 2021
Bangkok, Thailand (online)

Introduction

The MWE 2021 workshop (MWE 2021)[1] took place in an online format on August 6, 2021 in conjunction with ACL-IJCNLP 2021[2]. This was the 17th edition of the Workshop on Multiword Expressions (MWE 2021). The event was organized and sponsored by the Special Interest Group on the Lexicon (SIGLEX)[3] of the Association for Computational Linguistics (ACL).

Multiword expressions (MWEs) are word combinations, such as *in the middle of nowhere*, *hot dog*, *to make a decision* or *to kick the bucket*, displaying lexical, syntactic, semantic, pragmatic and/or statistical idiosyncrasies. Because of their unpredictable behavior, notably their non-compositional semantics, MWEs pose problems in linguistic modelling (e.g. treebank annotation, grammar engineering), Natural Language Processing (NLP) pipelines (in particular when orchestrated with parsing), and end-user NLP applications such as natural language understanding, machine translation, information extraction, and social media mining.

The special topic in this edition was the role of MWEs in end-user applications. On the one hand, the PARSEME shared tasks (Ramisch et al. 2020[4], Ramisch et al. 2018[5], Savary et al. 2017[6]), among others, fostered significant progress in MWE identification, providing datasets, evaluation measures and tools that now allow fully integrating MWE identification into end-user applications. On the other hand, NLP seems to be shifting towards end-to-end neural models capable of solving complex end-user tasks with little or no intermediary linguistic symbols, questioning the extent to which MWEs should be implicitly or explicitly modelled. Therefore, one goal of this workshop was to bring together and encourage researchers in various NLP subfields to submit MWE-related research, so that approaches that deal with MWEs in various applications could benefit from each other.

Traditional MWE topics

- Computationally-applicable theoretical work on MWEs and constructions in psycholinguistics and corpus linguistics
- MWE and construction annotation and representation in resources such as corpora, treebanks, e-lexicons and WordNets
- Processing of MWEs and constructions in syntactic and semantic frameworks (e.g. CCG, CxG, HPSG, LFG, TAG, UD, etc.)
- Discovery and identification methods for MWEs and constructions
- MWEs and constructions in language acquisition, language learning, and non-standard language (e.g. tweets, speech)
- Evaluation of annotation and processing techniques for MWEs and constructions
- Retrospective comparative analyses from the PARSEME shared tasks on automatic identification of MWEs

Topics on MWEs and end-user applications

- Processing of MWEs and constructions in end-user applications (e.g. MT, NLU, summarisation, social media mining, computer assisted language learning)

---

[1] https://multiword.org/mwe2021/

[2] https://2021.aclweb.org/

[3] https://siglex.org/

[4] https://www.aclweb.org/anthology/2020.mwe-1.14/

[5] https://www.aclweb.org/anthology/W18-4925/

[6] https://www.aclweb.org/anthology/W17-1704/

- Implicit and explicit representation of MWEs and constructions in end-user applications
- Evaluation of end-user applications concerning MWEs and constructions
- Resources and tools for MWEs and constructions (e.g. lexicons, identifiers) in end-user applications

Pursuing the MWE Section's tradition of synergies with other communities and in accordance with ACL-IJCNLP 2021's theme track on NLP for social good, a joint discussion panel was organized with the Workshop on Online Abuse and Harm (WOAH)[7].

This year, we received 19 submissions, among which 7 were accepted for presentation. The overall acceptance rate was 36%. In addition to the presentations, the workshop featured an invited talk that was given by Vered Shwartz, University of Washington.

We are grateful to the paper authors for their valuable contributions, the members of the Program Committee for their thorough and timely reviews, all members of the organizing committee for the fruitful collaboration, and all the workshop participants for their interest in this event. Our thanks also go to the ACL-IJCNLP 2021 organizers for their support, as well as to SIGLEX for their endorsement.

Paul Cook, Jelena Mitrović, Carla Parra Escartín, Ashwini Vaidya, Petya Osenova, Shiva Taslimipoor, Carlos Ramisch

---

[7]https://www.workshopononlineabuse.com/

Organizers

Program Chairs

Paul Cook, University of New Brunswick (Canada)
Jelena Mitrović, University of Passau (Germany)
Carla Parra Escartín, Iconic Translation Machines, Ltd. (Ireland)
Ashwini Vaidya, Indian Institute of Technology in Delhi (India)

Publication chairs

Petya Osenova, Institute of Information and Communication Technologies (Bulgaria)
Shiva Taslimipoor, University of Cambridge (UK)

Communication chair

Carlos Ramisch, Aix Marseille University (France)

Program Committee

Margarita Alonso-Ramos, Universidade da Coruña (Spain)
Tim Baldwin, University of Melbourne (Australia)
Verginica Barbu Mititelu, Romanian Academy (Romania)
Fabienne Cap, Uppsala University (Sweden)
Anastasia Christofidou, Academy of Athens (Greece)
Ken Church, IBM Research (USA)
Matthieu Constant, Université de Lorraine (France)
Monika Czerepowicka, University of Warmia and Mazury (Poland)
Myriam de Lhonneux, University of Copenhagen (Denmark)
Gaël Dias, University of Caen Basse-Normandie (France)
Meghdad Farahmand, University of Geneva (Switzerland)
Christiane Fellbaum, Princeton University (USA)
Joaquim Ferreira da Silva, New University of Lisbon (Portugal)
Karën Fort, Sorbonne Université (France)
Aggeliki Fotopoulou, ILSP/RC "Athena" (Greece)
Marcos Garcia, University of Santiago de Compostela (Spain)
Voula Giouli, Institute for Language and Speech Processing (Greece)
Stefan Th. Gries, University of California (USA)
Bruno Guillaume, Université de Lorraine (France)
Chikara Hashimoto, Yahoo!Japan (Japan)
Uxoa Iñurrieta, University of the Basque Country (Spain)
Diptesh Kanojia, IIT Bombay (India)
Elma Kerz, RWTH Aachen (Germany)
Ekaterina Kochmar, University of Cambridge (UK)
Dimitrios Kokkinakis, University of Gothenburg (Sweden)
Ioannis Korkontzelos, Edge Hill University (UK)
Cvetana Krstev, University of Belgrade (Serbia)
Eric Laporte, University Paris-Est Marne-la-Vallee (France)
Timm Lichte, University of Duesseldorf (Germany)
Teresa Lynn, ADAPT Centre (Ireland)

Stella Markantonatou, Institute for Language and Speech Processing (Greece)
Yuji Matsumoto, Nara Institute of Science and Technology (Japan)
Nurit Melnik, The Open University of Israel (Israel)
Laura A. Michaelis, University of Colorado Boulder (USA)
Johanna Monti, "L'Orientale" University of Naples (Italy)
Preslav Nakov, Qatar Computing Research Institute, HBKU (Qatar)
Malvina Nissim, University of Groningen (Netherlands)
Diarmuid Ó Séaghdha, University of Cambridge (UK)
Jan Odijk, University of Utrecht (Netherlands)
Haris Papageorgiou, Institute for Language and Speech Processing (Greece)
Marie-Sophie Pausé, independent researcher (France)
Pavel Pecina, Charles University (Czech Republic)
Ted Pedersen, University of Minnesota (USA)
Scott Piao, Lancaster University (UK)
Maciej Piasecki, Wroclaw University of Technology (Poland)
Alain Polguère, Université de Lorraine (France)
Matīss Rikters, University of Tokyo (Japan)
Fatiha Sadat, Université du Québec à Montréal (Canada)
Manfred Sailer, Goethe-Universität Frankfurt am Main (Germany)
Magali Sanches Duran, University of São Paulo (Brazil)
Branislava Šandrih, University of Belgrade (Serbia)
Agata Savary, Université François Rabelais Tours (France)
Sabine Schulte im Walde, University of Stuttgart (Germany)
Matthew Shardlow, Manchester Metropolitan University (UK)
Vered Shwartz, Allen AI (USA)
Gyri Smørdal Losnegaard, University of Bergen (Norway)
Ranka Stanković, University of Belgrade (Serbia)
Ivelina Stoyanova, Bulgarian Academy of Sciences (Bulgaria)
Stan Szpakowicz, University of Ottawa (Canada)
Carole Tiberius, Dutch Language Institute (Netherlands)
Beata Trawinski, Institut für Deutsche Sprache Mannheim (Germany)
Ruben Urizar, University of the Basque Country (Spain)
Aline Villavicencio, Federal University of Rio Grande do Sul (Brazil)
Veronika Vincze, Hungarian Academy of Sciences (Hungary)
Martin Volk, University of Zürich (Switzerland)
Zeerak Waseem, University of Sheffield (UK)
Eric Wehrli, University of Geneva (Switzerland)
Seid Muhie Yimam, Universität Hamburg (Germany)

Invited Speaker

Vered Shwartz, University of Washington

Table of Contents

Workshop Program

August 6, 2021
[All times are in CEST (UTC+2)]

14:00–14:10   **Welcome and Preparation**

14:10–15:50   **Session 1: Long Papers**
14:10–14:30   *Where Do Aspectual Variants of Light Verb Constructions Belong?*
Aggeliki Fotopoulou, Eric Laporte and Takuya Nakamura

14:30–14:50   *Data-driven Identification of Idioms in Song Lyrics*
Miriam Amin, Peter Fankhauser, Marc Kupietz and Roman Schneider

14:50–15:10   *(From Findings of ACL 2021) Transforming Term Extraction: Transformer-Based Approaches to Multilingual Term Extraction Across Domains*
Christian Lang, Lennart Wachowiak, Barbara Heinisch, Dagmar Gromann

15:10–15:30   *Contextualized Embeddings Encode Monolingual and Cross-lingual Knowledge of Idiomaticity*
Samin Fakharian and Paul Cook

15:30–15:50   *PIE: A Parallel Idiomatic Expression Corpus for Idiomatic Sentence Generation and Paraphrasing*
Jianing Zhou, Hongyu Gong and Suma Bhat

15:50–16:05   **Break**

16:05–17:05   **Invited Talk**
16:05–17:05   *A Long Hard Look at MWEs in the Age of Language Models*
Vered Shwartz

17:05–17:20   **Break**

17:20–18:05   **Session 2: Short Papers**
17:20–17:35   *Lexical Semantic Recognition*
Nelson F. Liu, Daniel Hershcovich, Michael Kranzlein and Nathan Schneider

17:35–17:50   *Finding BERT's Idiomatic Key*
Vasudevan Nedumpozhimana and John Kelleher

17:50–18:05   *Light Verb Constructions and Their Families - A Corpus Study on German 'stehen unter'-LVCs*
Jens Fleischhauer

18:05–18:20   **Break**

August 6, 2021 (continued)

18:20–19:00   Joint session with WOAH

19:00–19:20   Community discussion

A Long Hard Look at MWEs in the Age of Language Models

Vered Shwartz[1,2,3]
[1] Allen Institute for AI
[2] University of Washington
[3] University of British Columbia
vereds@allenai.org

Abstract

In recent years, language models (LMs) have become almost synonymous with NLP. Pre-trained to "read" a large text corpus, such models are useful as both a representation layer as well as a source of world knowledge. But how well do they represent MWEs?

This talk will discuss various problems in representing MWEs, and the extent to which LMs address them:

- Do LMs capture the implicit relationship between constituents in compositional MWEs (from *baby oil* through *parsley cake* to *cheeseburger stabbing*)?

- Do LMs recognize when words are used non-literally in non-compositional MWEs (e.g. do they know whether there are fleas in the *flea market*)?

- Do LMs know idioms, and can they infer the meaning of new idioms from the context as humans often do?

Bio

Vered Shwartz is a postdoctoral researcher at the Allen Institute for AI (AI2) and the University of Washington. She will join the Department of Computer Science at the University of British Columbia as an Assistant Professor in fall 2021. Her research interests include computational semantics and pragmatics, multiword expressions, and commonsense reasoning.

1

Where Do Aspectual Variants of Light Verb Constructions Belong?

Aggeliki Fotopoulou
ILSP, Athena RC
15125, Marousi, Greece

afotop@athenarc.gr

Eric Laporte   **Takuya Nakamura**
LIGM, Univ Gustave Eiffel, CNRS, ESIEE Paris
F-77454 Marne-la-Vallée, France
{eric.laporte, takuya.nakamura}@
univ-eiffel.fr

Abstract

Expressions with an aspectual variant of a light verb, e.g. *take on debt* vs. *have debt*, are frequent in texts but often difficult to classify between verbal idioms, light verb constructions or compositional phrases. We investigate the properties of such expressions with a disputed membership and propose a selection of features that determine more satisfactory boundaries between the three categories in this zone, assigning the expressions to one of them.

1   Introduction

An aspectual variant of a light verb or support verb (LV)[1] is a verb that contributes an aspectual meaning when substituted for a LV, as *take on debt* vs. *have debt*. Expressions with such verbs are frequent in texts but often difficult to classify between verbal idioms (VI), light verb constructions (LVC) or fully compositional phrases (CP), even following carefully the PARSEME guidelines for corpus annotation (Ramisch et al., 2020). In this paper, we focus on French expressions comprising (i) a verb that can be an aspectual variant of a LV in some contexts, and (ii) a single dependent of this verb, either direct: *prendre garde* (lit. 'take vigilance') 'be careful', *prendre une décision* (lit. 'take a decision') 'make a decision', *prendre conscience* (lit. 'take awareness') 'get aware', or prepositional: *prendre en compte* 'take into account', *entrer en discussion* 'enter into talks'. We investigate the properties of such expressions with a disputed membership and propose a selection of features that determine more satisfactory boundaries between the three categories in this zone,

assigning the expressions to one of them. In the next section, we survey related work. Section 3 lists the main features felt as relevant to the VI/LVC/CP distinction for the expressions at stake. In Section 4, we define two sets of expressions, and in Sections 5 and 6, we discuss their membership based on their features. The paper ends with concluding remarks.

2   Related work

Aspectual variants of light verb constructions, e.g. (fr) *prendre une couleur* (lit. 'take a colour') 'take on some colour' vs. *avoir une couleur* 'have some colour', are investigated by linguists from the beginning of the 1980s and often called 'extensions' of LVC (Vivès, 1984; Machonis, 1988; Gross, 1998). The distinction between VI and LVC dates back to the same period (Gross, 1988). For an expression to be considered an extension of LVC instead of VI, Fotopoulou (1992) sets explicit requirements that relate to (i) the syntactic operation producing the expression from the LVC, and (ii) the LVC proper itself. Her method is applied recently in Fotopoulou, Giouli (2015) and Picoli et al. (2021).

For these authors, after Gross (1981), the notion of LVC encompasses any construction where the main predicate is borne by a lexical unit distinct from the main verb, namely the noun *couleur* 'colour' in our example. Thus, a 2-argument predicate appears as a verb in (1), a noun in (2) and an adjective (*Adj*) in (3):

(1)   *The Kia differs from the Ford*
(2)   *The Kia has a difference with the Ford*
(3)   *The Kia is different from the Ford*

When the predicate is an *Adj*, the LV is a copula (Gross, 1981; Ranchhod, 1983; Cattell, 1984; Danlos, 1992; Laporte, 2018). If the predicate is a noun, it can be a direct object of the LV, but with some LV, it is a prepositional object (Gross,

---

[1] We will not make a difference between these two terms, because the way authors use them is not consistently correlated with differences between notions or approaches.

Proceedings of the 17th Workshop on Multiword Expressions, pages 2–12
Bangkok, Thailand (online), August 6, 2021. ©2021 Association for Computational Linguistics

1981), as in (fr) *procéder à une étude de* (lit. 'operate to a study of') 'carry out a study of' (LVC-annotated in the PARSEME corpus), parallel to *faire une étude de* 'make a study of'. Computational linguists' interest for LVC in the last 20 years has remained mainly limited to the prototypical case where the predicate is a noun in the position of an object of the verb, and where the semantic weight of the verb is minimal, but other types of LVC will inevitably prove relevant to applications.

In the framework of computational linguists' interest for MWE, Sag et al. (2002) classify LVC among syntactically flexible lexicalized MWE. The idea that LVC are not fully compositional is explained by the strong distributional constraints between the LV and the predicate. For example, *have some colour* and *carry out a study* are LVC, whereas **carry out a colour* does not make sense, and *have some study* is a CP, i.e. a combination only restricted by constraints specific to its components, each of which retains a meaning it has in other contexts, here *have* as 'own' or 'hold'. For Mel'čuk (2012), LVC are fully compositional collocations, and the distributional constraints between the LV and the predicate are specific features of the predicate, in the same way as the selection of the preposition *on* is a feature of the verb *depend* in *Our future depends on libraries*. In this paper, we stick to the current mainstream terminology where LVC are MWE, and we use 'CP' as an equivalent to 'non-MWE'.

The boundaries between VI, LVC and CP are considered a problem, but this problem is rarely addressed. Tu (2012) uses supervised learning, but does not investigate the linguistic criteria used to annotate the corpus. The PARSEME guidelines for annotation of verbal MWE in corpora (Ramisch et al., 2020), partially reproduced in Fig. 1, take into account many languages and the views of a broad group of researchers, and are a milestone on the path to delimitations based on criteria. However, aspectual variants of LVC are not handled in a completely consistent way, which motivates the present research.

3 Survey of relevant features

We briefly survey the main five features that have been invoked for the VI/LVC/CP distinction and are relevant to expressions with aspectual verbs.

3.1 Semantic contribution of the verb

The semantic contribution of the verb in the expression may be 'light', i.e. restricted to what is expressed by its inflectional features, as in *have debt,* or consist in some specific meaning, as in *take on debt*, where *take on* adds an aspectual meaning of beginning. This feature (test LVC.3, cf. Fig. 1) depends on the phrase: the same verb can add an aspectual meaning in a context, e.g. *take a prominent place*, and not in another, e.g. *take a walk.*

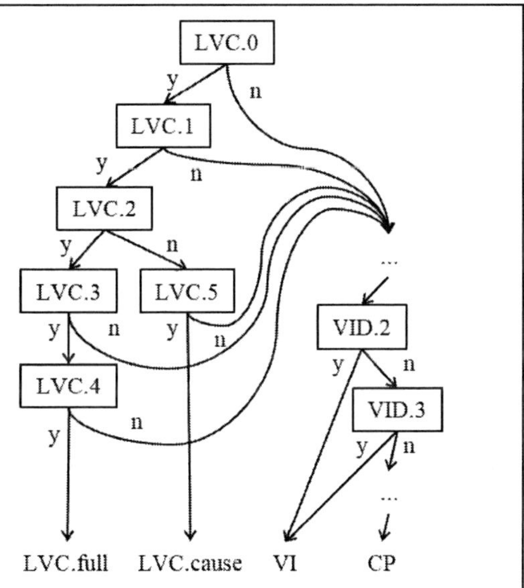

LVC.0: is the noun abstract?
LVC.1: is the noun predicative?
LVC.2: is the subject of the verb a semantic argument of the noun?
LVC.3: does the verb only add meaning expressed as morphological features?
LVC.4: can a verbless NP-reduction refer to the same event/state?
LVC.5: is the subject of the verb the cause of the noun?
VID.2: regular replacement of a component ⇒ unexpected meaning shift?
VID.3: regular morphological change ⇒ unexpected meaning shift?

Fig. 1. Excerpt of the PARSEME decision tree

3.2 Equivalence with a part of the phrase

In some verbal phrases such as *take a walk*, the predicative meaning of the complete phrase is also observed in a subphrase, here *walk*, and the arguments remain unchanged, as shown by comparing *The woman took a walk* and *the woman's walk*. In others, the predicative meaning requires the complete phrase: the idiomatic meaning in *Those dreams take flesh* 'Those dreams become real' can be observed with *take* or *give*, but not in a verbless noun phrase with *flesh* such as *the flesh of those dreams*.[2] The subphrase that retains the predicative meaning can be the phrase deprived of the verb, as in *take a walk*, or of both the verb and a preposition, as in *be in talks*: *The companies were in talks / the companies' talks*.

This property (test LVC.4) does not consist in mere semantic similarity between the phrase and the subphrase. In (fr) *prendre ses responsabilités* (lit. 'take one's responsibilities') 'face up to one's responsibilities', the complete phrase involves a voluntary attitude, in contrast with *responsabilités* 'responsibility' in other contexts, which denotes a situation.

3.3 Distributional constraints

Replacing a component of a MWE by related words may lead either to expected results, as in *have some* (*colour + shape + size + smell*), or to unexpected results (test VID.2), as in *take turns* 'alternate one's roles' vs. *take* (?*alternations + ?times + opportunities*).

3.4 Inflectional constraints

Changing the inflectional features of a component of a MWE may lead to expected results, as in *have some* (*colour + colours*), or to unexpected results (VID.3), as in *take turns* 'alternate one's roles' vs. *take a turn* 'take a walk'.

3.5 Typical verb alternations

Some verb alternations are known to produce an aspectual change, e.g. *have/take* in *have power/ take power*, or *have/gain, have/keep, have/lose, have regain, make/start, undergo/fall under*...

4 Scope of the paper

French verbs such as *entamer* 'start', *entrer* 'enter', *prendre* 'take', *tomber* 'fall', *conserver* 'preserve', *garder* 'keep', *perdre* 'lose', *sortir* 'get out', *retrouver* 'regain', *multiplier* 'multiply'... have been described as aspectual variants of LV. Expressions with such verbs pose more or less

difficult challenges to the VI/LVC/CP distinction. In this section, we put aside two types that do not pose classification problems, then we identify two sets of expressions that do. For consistency with related work, we use the tests in the PARSEME guidelines whenever possible.

First, some phrases like *prendre en compte* 'take into account' are reasonably easily analysed as VI, as showing distributional constraints (cf. 3.3) and no relation with any LVC. The meaning of *prendre ses responsabilités* (lit. 'take one's responsibilities') 'face up to one's responsibilities' changes unexpectedly if we replace the noun with related words: e.g. *prendre ses engagements* (lit. 'take one's commitments') means 'make one's commitments', not 'face up to one's commitments', and **prendre ses obligations* (lit. 'take one's duties') does not make sense. This observation characterizes *prendre ses responsabilités* as a VI. The meaning of *prendre garde* (lit. 'take vigilance') 'be careful' also changes unexpectedly in case of lexical substitutions, and differs from that of the two LVC *avoir la garde* 'have custody' and *avoir Det garde* 'have Det posture', a term of martial arts; thus, *prendre garde* is annotated as VI in the PARSEME corpus.

We also exclude from this paper the phrases that qualify as LVC.full by satisfying all the PARSEME tests until LVC.4, e.g. *prendre un bain* (lit. 'take a bath') 'have a bath'. This includes positivity to test LVC.3, which entails that the verb of these phrases does not add any aspectual meaning to the noun. Phrases such as *prendre un bain* 'have a bath' are consensually classified as LVC.

We now move on to phrases where the verb adds an aspectual meaning.

4.1 *Stricto sensu* aspectual variants of LVC

These are the phrases that qualify as input for PARSEME test LVC.3, but are negative to it since they add an aspectual meaning to the predicative noun, e.g. *prendre conscience* (lit. 'take awareness') 'become aware', *entrer en conflit* (lit. 'enter into conflict') 'enter into a conflict', *entamer une carrière* 'start a career' (Section 5).

4.2 Aspectual variants of prepositional-phrase idioms

The PARSEME guidelines restrict the notion of LVC to when the noun by itself is predicative (Ramisch et al., 2020). This excludes phrases such

---

[2] Or as a creative 'exploitation', not a lexicalized 'norm' in the sense of Hanks (2013).

as (fr) *entrer en vigueur* (lit. 'enter into vigour') 'come into force, become legally valid', since its idiomatic meaning is not observed without the preposition *en* (cf. 3.2), e.g. not in [?]*la vigueur de ce règlement* (lit. 'the vigour of this regulation'). We define our second set of expressions as those that:

(i) contain a non-compositional prepositional phrase (PP) with an idiomatic meaning that requires the preposition;

(ii) contain a verb that adds an aspectual meaning to the PP;

(iii) satisfy tests like LVC.0–2, but applied to the PP instead of the noun, i.e.: the PP is abstract (LVC.0bis) and predicative (LVC.1bis), and the subject of the verb is a semantic argument of the PP (LVC.2bis).

We study them in Section 6.

5   *Stricto sensu* aspectual LVC variants

5.1   Significance

Stricto sensu aspectual variants of LVC are common in texts. In most occurrences, the notion added by the verb is that of **beginning**, as in *prendre conscience* (lit. 'take awareness') 'become aware', *entrer en conflit* 'enter into a conflict'. The verb-related aspect can also be that of **regaining**, as in *retrouver sa vitalité* 'regain one's vitality', of **cessation** or termination, as in *abandonner son exigence* 'give up one's requirement', of **duration**, as in *conserver le souvenir* 'keep the memory', or of **repetition**, as in *multiplier les allusions* (lit. 'multiply the allusions') 'keep alluding'.

5.2   Subtypes

All these phrases have something in common, and in practice, applying the PARSEME guidelines, most of them end up labelled as compositional. However, in the PARSEME corpus, a small proportion are classified VI or LVC. In the former case (VI), the reasons for this labelling may have been **number constraints** (test VID.3), as in **prendre** *une* **place** *prépondérante* '**take** a prominent **place**', where the noun is always in the singular, or **lexical constraints** (test VID.2), as in *tomber en panne* (lit. 'fall into breakdown') 'break down, get out of order', where replacing *tomber* or *panne* with semantically related words like *problème* 'problem' may produce unexpected results such as with **tomber en problème*. How

do *stricto sensu* aspectual variants of LVC behave in terms of morphological and lexical constraints? Is their behaviour a reason to make distinctions between them?

5.3   Number constraints

The number constraint (mandatory singular) in *prendre une place Adj* 'take an *Adj* place' is a valid motivation for the VI label. However, the same constraint is also observed in many phrases that are not labelled VI or LVC in the PARSEME corpus, which amounts to analysing them as compositional (CP), e.g. *prendre une importance Adj* (lit. 'take an importance *Adj*') 'take on *Adj* importance', which is strikingly similar to *prendre une place Adj*. Here are other CP-labelled examples positive to test VID.3, with the singular: *perdre de son importance* (lit. 'lose of one's importance') 'lose some importance', *prendre l'habitude de* (lit. 'take the habit of') 'get used to', *tomber en désuétude* 'fall into disuse', *retrouver sa vitalité* 'regain one's vitality', *entrer en conflit* 'enter into a conflict', *prendre le pouvoir* (lit. 'take the power') 'take power'. Most occurrences with the constraint of a noun mandatorily in the plural are also analysed as CP, e.g. *multiplier les revendications / manifestations / allusions* (lit. 'multiply the demands / demonstrations / allusions') 'keep demanding/demonstrating/alluding'.

According to the guidelines, these number restrictions assign the expressions to category VI, but the annotators of the corpus did not take them into account, maybe due to a feeling that they arise from general grammar rules. This discrepancy between guidelines and practice, and also the few cases where the number restrictions did lead to VI labellings, may be a sign of a problem in the guidelines.

The problem may be that *stricto sensu* aspectual variants of LVC are processed differently from LVC proper. As a matter of fact, the constraint of a noun mandatorily in the singular is common in LVC, e.g. in *avoir une place Adj* 'have a *Adj* place', *avoir une importance Adj* 'have *Adj* importance', *avoir l'habitude de* (lit. 'have the habit of') 'be used to', *être en désuétude* 'be in disuse', *avoir de la vitalité* 'have some vitality', *avoir le pouvoir* (lit. 'have the power') 'have power'... In these LVC, the noun always occurs in the singular. This syntactic feature of these nouns is not a reason to analyse the phrases as VI. In the case of *avoir l'habitude de* (lit. 'have the habit of') 'be used to', the number constraint is relaxed if the second argument is not explicitly expressed:

(4) **Le garçonnet a les habitudes de sortir et de jouer*

      (lit. 'The boy has the habits of going out and playing')

(5) *Le garçonnet a de nouvelles habitudes*

      'The boy has new habits'

The predicative meaning of *avoir Det habitude* is the same in both cases,[3] and it would be absurd to analyse the phrase as an idiom or a LVC depending on whether the second argument is expressed or not.

The PARSEME guidelines are consistent with the view that number constraints are not a reason to analyse LVC as VI. As the LVC are positive to test LVC.3 ('the verb only adds meaning expressed as morphological features'), the guidelines don't test VID.3, which amounts to considering number restrictions as an effect of general grammar rules, and therefore these phrases do not get a VI labelling. In contrast, their aspectual counterparts such as *prendre une place Adj*, which are negative to LVC.3, are sent to the VID-specific subtree, where they are tested for number restrictions like *kick the* (*bucket* + **buckets*), and in principle end up annotated as VI. But there is no particular reason to think that the number constraint is an effect of general rules in *avoir une place Adj* and not in *prendre une place Adj*.

Therefore, we suggest the decision tree should take into account the similarity between the LVC and their aspectual variants, by establishing a subtree without test VID.3 for LVC.3-negative expressions adding an aspectual meaning to the noun, just like the category of causal LVC (LVC.cause) defined in the PARSEME guidelines.

5.4 Lexical constraints

The other reason to annotate aspectual variants of LVC as VI was test VID.2 (restrictions to lexical substitution). Are these distributional constraints a reason to analyse the phrases as idioms?

Take the example of *tomber en panne* (lit. 'fall into breakdown') 'break down', annotated VI in the PARSEME corpus. A large class of nouns can be substituted for *panne*, among them *admiration* 'admiration', *désaccord* 'disagreement', *émer-*

veillement 'awe', with regular semantic effects. These nouns are semantically related or unrelated to *panne*, but all occur in LVC with *avoir* 'have', like *panne* does in *avoir une panne* (lit. 'have a breakdown') 'be out of order'. And a few verbs commute with *tomber*: mainly *être* 'be', *rester* 'remain', *demeurer* 'remain'.

The case of *entrer en discussion* 'enter into talks' is quite similar, although it is annotated as CP in the corpus. *Discussion* can be replaced by many nouns, including *conflit* 'conflict', *conformité* 'compliance', *décomposition* 'decay', and also the nouns cited above about *tomber en panne*; they are semantically related or unrelated to *discussion*, but all occur in LVC with *avoir* 'have' or *mener* 'lead', like *discussion* in *avoir des discussions* 'have talks' and *mener des dicussions* (lit. 'lead talks') 'hold talks'. But the same few verbs as above commute with *entrer*: *être* 'be', *rester* 'remain', *demeurer* 'remain'.

In both *tomber en panne* and *entrer en discussion*, the possibilities of substitution of the noun involve nouns occurring in LVC with the same LV; and the possibilities of substitution of the verb are limited to a small number of common verbs. This similarity between *tomber en panne* and *entrer en discussion* extends not only to most aspectual variants of LVC, e.g. *prendre le pouvoir* (lit. 'take the power') 'take power', but more importantly to LVC proper themselves. For example, in the LVC *avoir une panne* (lit. 'have a breakdown') 'be out of order', *panne* shows ample possibilities of substitution, while *avoir* commutes only with *connaître* 'know', *présenter* 'show', *subir* 'undergo'.

The situation is the same as in 5.3: in LVC, the LV has limited possibilities of substitution, but that does not lead to analyse the phrases as VI, and there are no particular reasons to think that similar distributional constraints should motivate another model for *tomber en panne* than for *avoir une panne*. In other words, the possibilities of substitution for each item in the (aspectual verb / noun) pair is more typical of a (LV/noun) pair like *have a talk* than of two components in a VI like *hit the roof* 'get angry'. This is a second point in support of a specific subtree, without test VID.2, for LVC.3-negative expressions adding an aspectual meaning to the noun.

---

[3] *Det* stands for 'determiner'.

5.5 Judging the meaning added by the verb

In the PARSEME corpus, a small proportion of *stricto sensu* aspectual variants of LVC are classified LVC. The aspectual contribution of the verb in these phrases is slight, as in *garder le silence* (lit. 'keep the silence') 'stand mute', or has been overlooked during application of test LVC.3: *prendre position* (lit. 'take position') 'take up position'. These disparities suggest a lack of reliability of this test.

Despite appearances, the 'meaning added' by a word to another, as in test LVC.3, is difficult to observe reproducibly, and even more if the word is a verb. A word or sequence of words acquires a precise meaning only in a context. In practice, comparing a noun like *position* with a verb/noun sequence like *prendre position* is not straight-forward because they are not used in the same syntactic contexts. Thus, this test, if applied as such, inevitably involves, on the one hand, an informal survey of comparable contexts for the noun and for the verb/noun sequence, and on the other hand, a comparison of the meanings of these contexts. In these mental operations, the judge may unconsciously blend relevant and irrelevant senses, e.g. 'location', 'military position', 'point of view'... in the case of (fr) *position*, and thus form a semantically imprecise mental image of the word. In addition, a comparison between several contexts of one form and several contexts of another involves many pairs of forms, and again some averaging. The resulting decision is bound to be highly dependent on the judge.

But a more practical and reliable procedure is often applicable, using the fact that the noun is predicative (LVC.1) and its arguments are supposed to be identifiable (LVC.2). In such a case, the predicative noun can usually occur with all its arguments in a LVC in the sense of the PARSEME guidelines, i.e. positive to tests LVC.0–4, e.g. *avoir une position [militaire]* (lit. 'have a position') 'hold a position'. Indeed, at least in Romance languages where LVC have been extensively studied, few examples of predicative nouns that do not occur in a LVC proper are known, maybe *départ* 'departure' and *arrivée* 'arrival'. Checks can be applied to the phrase under study (in our example, *prendre position*) and to the LVC in order to make sure that the noun predicate retains the same sense and the same inventory of arguments, and that the distribution of each argument remains the same:

(6) *Osburn prend position dans Thulin*
    (lit. 'Osburn takes position in Thulin')
    'Osburn takes up position in Thulin'

The aspectual variant has two arguments: the military and the location, just like the LVC:

(7) *Osburn a une position dans Thulin*
    (lit. 'Osburn has a position in Thulin')
    'Osburn holds a position in Thulin'

Whenever a LVC with the noun has been identified, a comparison with the phrase under study (*prendre position*) is more reproducibly observable than the current LVC.3 approach, because each term of the comparison is a predicate with its arguments, i.e. almost a sentence, which identifies a precise sense. And the comparison targets precisely the semantic difference resulting from the substitution of the verb under study for a LV *stricto sensu*. Examples are *garder le silence* (lit. 'keep the silence') 'stand mute', *rester dans le silence* (lit. 'remain in the silence') 'remain in silence', *sortir du silence* 'get out of the silence'. The phrases *tomber en panne* (lit. 'fall into breakdown') 'break down', *entrer en discussion* 'enter into talks', *tomber sous l'influence* 'fall under the influence', and many other aspectual phrases with a motion verb, have in common the fact that a LVC with *être* 'be' and a preposition[4] can be used for the comparison (Danlos, 1988): *être en panne* (lit. 'be in breakdown') 'be out of order', *être en discussion* 'be in talks', *être sous l'influence* 'be under the influence'. The PARSEME corpus systematically labels such LVC as CP, but they satisfy the PARSEME guidelines for LVC proper, and they have equivalents with transitive LV: *avoir une panne* (lit. 'have a breakdown') 'be out of order', *avoir une discussion* 'have a talk', *subir l'influence* 'undergo the influence'. These constructions with *être* 'be' are more frequent than those with transitive verbs, and show richer syntactic flexibility, since *être* also behaves as a copula:

(8) *un pays socialiste (qui est) sous l'influence de l'URSS*

    'a socialist country (that is) under the influence of the USSR'

Recapitulating: in test LVC.3, to increase the reproducibility of the decision, we suggest a methodological change: searching first for some

---

[4] The preposition in use with *être* is the same as with the aspectual verb, except in the case of cessative verbs: *sortir de l'influence* 'get out of the influence' vs. *être sous l'influence* 'be under the influence'.

LVC with the same noun predicate and arguments. If such a LVC is in use, the 'meaning added by the verb' will be identified as the semantic difference between the two constructions. If not, it will still be identified by semantic intuition, as in the current approach to LVC.3.

5.6 Relationship with LVC

Where do *stricto sensu* aspectual variants of LVC belong? The PARSEME guidelines generally analyse them as CP, which is understandable because both the verb and the predicate noun contribute to the meaning of the expression independently. This choice is compatible with our suggestion of a subtree for this type of phrase. However, the distributional constraints between the elements of the construction are more typical of LVC than of CP. An alternative option is to consider them as a category of LVC, like the category of causal LVC (LVC.cause) defined in the PARSEME guidelines.

First, a *stricto sensu* aspectual variant of LVC, as defined in Section 4.1, cannot be analysed as a combination of two predicates, since the aspectual verb does not introduce any specific argument. The inventory of arguments, and the selection of each argument, are the same as in the corresponding LVC, as in examples (6)-(7) above. In current computational models where words are represented by distributional data extracted from their contexts in corpora, an association between LVC and their aspectual variants is likely to help capturing their common distributional regularities.

Second, a given aspectual verb occurring in one of these phrases, as *prendre* 'take' in (6), does not combine with just any noun predicate: a selection operates between them. For example, *prendre* does not occur with *carrière* 'career' in an aspectual phrase, but *entamer* 'engage in' does:

(9) **Valli prend une carrière solo*

(lit. 'Valli takes a solo career')

(10) *Valli entame une carrière solo*

'Valli starts a solo career'

(On this point, aspectual variants of LV stand in contrast with aspectual auxiliary verbs such as *begin to* or *keep on*, which combine very freely with verbs.) In addition, noun predicates that occur in LVC with the same LV are more likely to combine with the same aspectual verbs. For instance, those with *avoir* 'have' often combine with *prendre* 'take', *entrer en* 'enter into' or *tomber en* 'fall into', while those with *faire* 'make' often combine with *entamer* 'engage in' or *multiplier* 'multiply'. Here again, corpus-driven representations are more likely to capture distributional regularities if the aspectual variant is processed like the LVC proper.

Another backbone of MWE processing is lexical databases (Savary et al., 2019). A lexical database can a priori encode the properties of the aspectual construction either in the entry of the aspectual verb, or in that of the noun predicate, or distribute them between both. However, due to the statistical regularities between types of aspectual constructions and types of LVC, the best solution is to encode them in the lexical entry of the noun predicate. This is equivalent to considering the aspectual construction as the result of a syntactic operation on the LVC, and therefore, as a part of the syntax of the noun.

This pairing between aspectual constructions and their corresponding LVC is a restriction to their compositionality, which makes the analysis as CP not entirely satisfactory. Creating an additional category for aspectual variants of LVC would make the classification of MWE even more complex than it already is. We suggest to consider them as a subtype of LVC, like the category of causal LVC (LVC.cause) in the PARSEME guidelines.

To do so, the decision tree can be adapted by assigning category LVC.asp to the phrases with negativity to LVC.3 when the semantic difference (beyond that expressed as morphological features) is in terms of aspect.

6 Aspectual variants of PP idioms

In phrases such as *entrer en vigueur* (lit. 'enter into vigour') 'come into force', the idiomatic meaning requires the preposition, i.e. it is not observed in [?]*la vigueur de ce règlement* (lit. 'the vigour of this regulation'). But the idiomatic meaning does not require the verb, since it is observed in *l'accord de pêche en vigueur* 'the fisheries agreement in force'; when the verb is present, it adds an aspectual meaning to the PP idiom, here a notion of change of state.

6.1 Subtypes

Since the noun in these phrases does not have the idiomatic meaning without the preposition, it is not predicative by itself. Consequently, these phrases can't satisfy test LVC.1 ('is the noun predicative?'), and the PARSEME guidelines do not classify them as LVC. Two other analyses are possible for these phrases. They contain an idiom which combines at least the preposition and the noun; if the verb is also considered as part of this idiom (i.e. the idiom in our example would be *entrer en vigueur* 'come into force'), the phrase is encoded as VI in the corpus; if it is not considered so (i.e., the idiom would be only *en vigueur* 'into force'), the phrase is left unannotated, since the annotation is limited to verbal MWE. We found only two VI-encoded occurrences of these phrases: *tomber aux mains* (lit. 'fall to the hands') 'fall into the hands' and *entrer en vigueur* (lit. 'enter into vigour') 'come into force', and many unannotated occurrences, e.g. *tomber entre les mains* (lit. 'fall between the hands') 'fall into the hands', *atterrir sur la place publique* (lit. 'land onto the town square') 'come to the public eye'.

The decision whether the verb is part of the idiom or not involves mainly lexical flexibility: does the verb commute with other verbs without unexpected changes in meaning? to what extent does the PP commute with other sequences without unexpected changes in meaning? For example, in the case of *entrer en vigueur*, the PP *en vigueur* can be replaced with *en application* (lit. 'in application') 'into force', *dans une impasse* 'into a deadlock', *en jeu* 'into play', etc. while the verb commutes mainly with *être* 'be', *rester* 'remain', *demeurer* 'remain'. In the case of *tomber entre les mains*, the PP *entre les mains* can be replaced with *dans le collimateur* (lit. 'into the collimator') 'into the cross hairs', *sous l'influence* 'under the influence', *à la merci* 'at the mercy', etc. while the verb commutes mainly with *être, rester, demeurer*. The distributional profiles of these two phrases do not show sufficient differences to justify the distinct encodings VI and CP. The situation is the same with other aspectual variants of PP: *rester en suspens* (lit. 'remain in irresolution') 'remain pending', *sortir de l'affiche* (lit. 'get out of the poster') 'cease to be on show'...

Thus, the idiomatic PP in these constructions commutes with many others, while the aspectual verb commutes with few common verbs. These facts remind those reported in 5.4: the possibilities of substitution for each item in the verb/PP pair are more typical of a (LV/noun) pair like *have a talk* than of two components in a verbal idiom like *hit the roof* 'get angry'. This distributional profile

supports an analysis of *entrer en vigueur* (lit. 'enter into vigour') 'come into force' where *en vigueur* 'in force' is an idiom, but *entrer* 'enter' is not part of the idiom.

6.2   Judging the meaning added by the verb

Our initial definition of aspectual variants of PP (Section 4.2) states that the verb 'adds an aspectual meaning to the PP'. This formulation shares the methodological flaw reported in Section 5.5: the meaning added by a word to a phrase is difficult to observe reproducibly, and all the more as the word is a verb. For instance, the meanings of *entrer en service* (lit. 'enter into service') 'begin to work' and *en service* (lit. 'in service') 'working' can hardly be compared reliably because these phrases are not used in the same syntactic contexts.

For more precision and reliability, we in fact compare the candidate phrase to a verbal phrase with the verb that has the least possible semantic content, here *être en service* (lit. 'be in service') 'be working'. For most if not all aspectual variants of PP, such a counterpart is obtained by substituting *être* 'be' for the aspectual verb, at least in Romance languages where PP idioms have been extensively studied: *être en vigueur* (lit. 'be in vigour') 'be in force', *être entre les mains* 'be in the hands'... The semantic emptiness of the verb *être* in such constructions can be checked by observing that it behaves as a copula:[5]

(11) *l'accord de pêche (qui est) en vigueur*

'the fisheries agreement (that is) in force'

By comparing the copular construction with the candidate phrase, one can check that the PP predicate retains the same sense and the same inventory of arguments, and that the distribution of each argument remains the same. The term of 'aspectual variant' is relevant only if the two constructions are parallel in all respects.

Similarly to what we noticed for phrases with a noun predicate, the preposition in use with the copula is the same as with the aspectual verb, except in the case of cessative verbs: *sortir de l'affiche* (lit. 'get out of the poster') 'cease to be on show' vs. *être à l'affiche* (lit. 'be at the poster') 'be on show'.

The PARSEME terminology restricts the term of LVC to noun predicates, but in the terminology

---

[5] Some linguists classify such PP as multiword adjectives (Danlos, 1981; Baldwin et al., 2006; Piunno, 2016; Piunno, Ganfi, 2020).

that calls LVC any sentence where the main predicate is borne by a lexical unit distinct from the main verb (cf. Section 2; Machonis, 1988; Vietri, 1996), *être en service* (lit. 'be in service') 'be working' is a LVC and *être* is a LV. As a matter of fact, if we substitute 'predicational form' for 'noun predicate' in the PARSEME tests, these copular constructions satisfy LVC.0–2. They consist of the LV *être* and a PP idiom embedded in the LVC.

Recapitulating: even if we do not use this terminology, an operational definition of aspectual variants of PP consists in searching first for some copular construction with the same PP and arguments. If such a construction is in use, the 'meaning added by the verb' will be identified as the semantic difference between the two constructions. If not, it will still be identified by semantic intuition, as in the current formulation of PARSEME test LVC.3.

6.3   Relationship with LVC

Where do aspectual variants of PP idioms belong? We have highlighted their similarity with *stricto sensu* aspectual variants of LVC (Section 5); the main difference is that the predicate is a PP idiom in the former and a noun in the latter. (This is not surprising: our delimitation of the two sets of phrases is entirely parallel.) They share several features:

(i) the verb adds an aspectual meaning to the predicate;

(ii) it does not introduce any specific argument;

(iii) the selection of the arguments of the predicate remains the same with or without the aspectual verb;

(iv) a given predicate may combine with several aspectual verbs, but not with any of them: a selection operates.

We suggested considering *stricto sensu* aspectual variants of LVC as a subtype of LVC (LVC.asp), like the category of causal LVC (LVC.cause) defined in the PARSEME guidelines. We noted that the term 'LVC' is relevant to constructions with a copula and a predicate. A consequence of these changes to the decision tree is that aspectual variants of PP idioms will be included in LVC.asp.

7   Conclusion

Aspectual variants of LVC are frequent in texts but have not been assigned a consensual place among the categories MWE, LVC or VI yet. The present work addresses this challenge by:

- defining two sets of expressions relevant to the problem,

- assessing the distributional variability of these expressions,

- taking into account relations between aspectual variants and LVC proper, i.e. LVC with a verbless variant.

A category of aspectual variants of LVC, like *prendre conscience* 'become aware', can be delimited on the following criterion: a construction is considered as such in case of a close relation with a LVC proper, here *avoir conscience* 'be aware', where the predicate/argument structure is preserved.

Due to the close similarity between the two types of constructions, aspectual variants of LVC could be considered as a special case of LVC, just like causal LVC are in the PARSEME guidelines.

Many PP idioms like *en vigueur* 'in force' can be analysed as predicational forms and are usable with a copula, which behaves as a LV. Such expressions, just like the LVC we just mentioned, often have aspectual variants like *entrer en vigueur* 'come into force'.

We gave our examples in French, but a similar behaviour of aspectual variants of LVC has been reported in Portuguese (Ranchhod, 1989, 1990; Baptista, 2005; Barros, 2014; Santos, 2015; Picoli et al., 2021), Italian (De Angelis, 1989; Vietri, 1996), Greek (Fotopoulou, 1992; Moustaki, 1995; Pantazara, 2003), and Spanish (Mogorrón, 1996; Blanco, Buvet, 2004). Our conclusions, both on aspectual variants of LVC and on PP idioms, are extensible to these languages, and maybe to English (Machonis, 1988; Garcia-Vega, Machonis, 2014), Romanian (Rădulescu, 1995), and Korean (Han, 2000, vol. 1, p. 123–126).

Acknowledgments

This work was supported by the French PARSEME-FR grant (ANR-14-CERA-0001). We are grateful to the anonymous reviewers for their useful comments.

References

Angela De Angelis. 1989. Nominalizations with Italian support verb *avere*. *Lingvisticae Investigationes*, 13(2):223–237. http://dx.doi.org/10.1075/li.13.2.02ang

Timothy Baldwin, John Beavers, Leonoor van der Beek, Francis Bond, Dan Flickinger, and Ivan A. Sag. 2006. In Search of a Systematic Treatment of Determinerless PPs. In *Computational Linguistics Dimensions of Syntax and Semantics of Prepositions*. Springer, pages 163–180.

Jorge Baptista. 2005. *Sintaxe dos predicados nominais com* ser de. Lisboa: Fundação Calouste Gulbenkian, Fundação para a Ciência e a Tecnologia.

Cláudia Dias de Barros. 2014. *Descrição e classificação de predicados nominais com o verbo-suporte* fazer. PhD, Universidade federal de São Carlos.

Xavier Blanco and Pierre-André Buvet. 2005. Verbes supports et significations grammaticales. Implications pour la traduction espagnol-français. *Lingvisticae Investigationes*, 27(2):327–342. https://doi.org/10.1075/li.27.2.13bla

Ray, Cattell. 1984. *Composite Predicates in English*. Academic Press.

Laurence Danlos. 1981. La morphosyntaxe des expressions figées. *Langages*, 63:53–74 and 127–128. https://doi.org/10.3406/lgge.1981.1876

Laurence Danlos. 1988. Les phrases à verbe support *être Prép. Langages*, 90:23–37. https://doi.org/10.3406/lgge.1988.1989

Laurence Danlos. 1992. Support verb constructions: linguistic properties, representation, translation. *Journal of French Language Studies*, 2(1):1–32. https://doi.org/10.1017/S0959269500001137

Vasiliki Foufi, Luka Nerima, and Eric Wehrli. 2017. Automatic Annotation of Verbal Collocations in Modern Greek. *Europhras*, pages 36–44. http://doi.org/10.26615/978-2-9701095-2-5_005

Angeliki Fotopoulou. 1992. Dictionnaires électroniques des phrases figées. Traitement d'un cas particulier: phrases figées/phrases à *Vsup*. In *COMPLEX. Papers in Computational Lexicography*. Hungarian Academy of Sciences, pages 147–161.

Angeliki Fotopoulou and Voula Giouli. 2015. MWEs: Support/light Verb Constructions vs. Fixed Expressions in Modern Greek and French. In *Workshop on Multiword units in machine translation and translation technology*. Tradulex, pages 68–73.

Michelle Garcia-Vega, Peter Machonis. 2014. The support verb *take*. In *Penser le Lexique-Grammaire. Perspectives actuelles*. Honoré Champion, pages 111–123.

Maurice Gross. 1981. Les bases empiriques de la notion de prédicat sémantique. *Langages*, 63:7–52 and 127–128. https://doi.org/10.3406/lgge.1981.1875

Maurice Gross. 1988. Les limites de la phrase figée. *Langages*, 90:7–22. https://doi.org/10.3406/lgge.1988.1988

Maurice Gross. 1998. La fonction sémantique des verbes supports. *Travaux de linguistique*, 37:25–46.

Sun-hae Han. 2000. *Les prédicats nominaux en coréen. Constructions à verbe support* hata. PhD, Université Paris 7.

Patrick Hanks. 2013. *Lexical Analysis: Norms and Exploitations*. Cambridge, MA: MIT Press.

Peter A. Machonis. 1988. Support verbs: an analysis of *be Prep X* idioms. *The SECOL Review*, 122:95–125.

Igor Mel'čuk. 2012. Phraseology in the language, in the dictionary, and in the computer. *Yearbook of Phraseology*, 3:31–56. https://doi.org/10.1515/phras-2012-0003

Pedro Mogorrón. 1996, Les expressions figées des verbes *ser* et *estar* suivies de *Prép X*, *Lingvisticae Investigationes*, 20(1):3–31. http://dx.doi.org/10.1075/li.20.1.03hue

Argyro Moustaki. 1997. Analyse contrastive des formes *être Prép X* en grec moderne et en français, *Lingvisticae Investigationes*, 21(1):29–73. http://dx.doi.org/10.1075/li.21.1.03mou

Andromaque-Virginie Pantazara. 2003. *Syntaxe dérivationnelle du grec moderne. Les constructions verbales à un complément prépositionnel et les constructions nominales et adjectivales prédicatives associées*. PhD, Université Paris 8.

Larissa Picoli, Oto A. Vale, and Eric Laporte. 2021. Aspecto verbal nas construções com verbo-suporte. *Revista do GEL*, 18(1):204–229. https://doi.org/10.21165/gel.v18i1.2897

Valentina Piunno. 2016. Multiword Modifiers in Romance languages. Semantic formats and syntactic templates. *Yearbook of Phraseology*, 7:3–34. https://doi.org/10.1515/phras-2016-0002

Valentina Piunno and Vittorio Ganfi. 2020. Synchronic and diachronic analysis of prepositional multiword modifiers across Romance languages. *Lingvisticae Investigationes*,

43(1):352–379.
https://doi.org/10.1075/li.00054.piu

Anda-Irina Rădulescu. 1995. Analyse contrastive des formes *être Prép X* en français et en roumain. *Lingvisticae Investigationes*, 19(2):289–324. https://doi.org/10.1075/li.19.2.05rad

Carlos Ramisch, Bruno Guillaume, Agata Savary, et al. 2020. *Annotated corpora and tools of the PARSEME Shared Task on Semi-Supervised Identification of Verbal Multiword Expressions (edition 1.2)*, LINDAT/CLARIAH digital library at the Institute of Formal and Applied Linguistics (ÚFAL), Faculty of Mathematics and Physics, Charles University. http://hdl.handle.net/11234/1-3367.

Elisabete Ranchhod. 1983. On the support verbs *ser* and *estar* in Portuguese. *Lingvisticae Investigationes*, 19(2):265–288. https://doi.org/10.1075/li.7.2.07ran

Elisabete Ranchhod. 1989. Lexique-grammaire du portugais. Prédicats nominaux supportés par *estar*. *Lingvisticae Investigationes*, 13(2):351–367. https://doi.org/10.1075/li.13.2.08ran

Elisabete Ranchhod. 1990. *Sintaxe dos Predicados Nominais com* Estar. Lisbon: Instituto Nacional de Investigação Científica.

Ivan A. Sag, Timothy Baldwin, Francis Bond, Ann Copestake, Dan Flickinger. 2002. Multiword Expressions: A Pain in the Neck for NLP. In *Proceedings of the 3rd International Conference on Intelligent Text Processing and Computational Linguistics (CICLing-2002)*. LNCS, 2276, Springer, pages 1–15. http://dx.doi.org/10.1007/3-540-45715-1_1

Maria Cristina dos Santos. 2015. *Descrição dos predicados nominais com o verbo-suporte* ter. PhD, Universidade federal de São Carlos.

Agata Savary, Silvio Cordeiro, and Carlos Ramisch. 2019. Without lexicons, multiword expression identification will never fly: A position statement. In *MWE-WN*, pages 79–91, Florence, Italy. ACL.

Yuancheng Tu. 2012. *English Complex Verb Constructions: Identification And Inference*. PhD, University of Illinois.

Simonetta Vietri. 1996. The syntax of the Italian verb *essere Prep. Lingvisticae Investigationes*, 20(2): 287–363. http://dx.doi.org/10.1075/li.20.2.04vie

Robert Vivès. 1984. L'aspect dans les constructions nominales prédicatives: *avoir, prendre,* verbe support et extension aspectuelle. *Lingvisticae Investigationes*, 8(1):161–185. http://doi.org/10.1075/li.8.1.11viv

Data-driven Identification of Idioms in Song Lyrics

Miriam Amin[1], Peter Fankhauser[2], Marc Kupietz[2], Roman Schneider[2]

[1]Leipzig University, Leipzig, Germany
`miriam_amin@web.de`
[2]Leibniz Institute For The German Language, Mannheim, Germany
`{fankhauser|kupietz|schneider}@ids-mannheim.de`

Abstract

The automatic recognition of idioms poses a challenging problem for NLP applications. Whereas native speakers can intuitively handle multiword expressions whose compositional meanings are hard to trace back to individual word semantics, there is still ample scope for improvement regarding computational approaches. We assume that idiomatic constructions can be characterized by gradual intensities of semantic non-compositionality, formal fixedness, and unusual usage context, and introduce a number of measures for these characteristics, comprising count-based and predictive collocation measures together with measures of context (un)similarity. We evaluate our approach on a manually labelled gold standard, derived from a corpus of German pop lyrics. To this end, we apply a Random Forest classifier to analyze the individual contribution of features for automatically detecting idioms, and study the trade-off between recall and precision. Finally, we evaluate the classifier on an independent dataset of idioms extracted from a list of Wikipedia idioms, achieving state-of-the art accuracy.

1 Introduction

Traditional accounts of idiomaticity distinguish idiomatic use of language from literal use, claiming that idioms are multiword expressions (MWEs) which do not conform to Frege's principle, i.e. whose meaning as a whole cannot fully be derived from the aggregated meaning of their components (Gibbon, 1982). In other words, the definition refers to non-compositionality and non-transparency – idiomatic MWEs seem semantically opaque; Baldwin and Kim (2010) consider this "lexical idiomaticity" to be one of five sub-types of idiomacity. Classifying idioms is not trivial: With reference to recent findings in discourse analysis and psycholinguistics, Wulff (2008) describes idiomati-

city as a non-binary, multifactorial concept for a "continuum ranging from clearly non-idiomatic patterns to core idioms"; Pradhan et al. (2018) support this observation experimentally. At least core idioms are considered to be (mentally) lexicalized: Schneider et al. (2014) describe them as "lexicalized combinations of two or more words" which, though often syntactically diverse, "are exceptional enough to be considered as individual units in the lexicon". This corresponds to Sinclair's idiom principle (Sinclair, 1991), postulating that text is often constructed from ready made phrases. Due to morphological and syntactic variation, the degree of formal fixedness ranges from semi- to fully-fixed. However, idiomaticity should be corpus-based verifiable, as e.g. Gries (2008, p. 22) states that "researchers interested in phraseologisms use frequencies and other more elaborated statistics" to identify "symbolic units and constructions". Some of these statistics may relate to local contexts, because one can reasonably argue that words that are not used literally will probably be somehow surprising in their context.

Against this background, we regard idioms as a subcategory of MWEs that are conspicuous in function, form and distribution – and with fuzzy boundaries to other multiword units like metaphors (Stefanowitsch and Gries, 2007) or proverbs. Our objective is to cover idiom characteristics with an innovative set of quantitative features, taking up some ideas described in the subsequent section, and to apply and evaluate machine-learning classifiers for a presumable idiomatically rich specialized corpus.

2 Related work

Idioms are a key concern and pose challenging problems for NLP applications such as information extraction, retrieval, summarization and translation, as well as for lexicographical studies or lan-

Proceedings of the 17th Workshop on Multiword Expressions, pages 13–22
Bangkok, Thailand (online), August 6, 2021. ©2021 Association for Computational Linguistics

guage learning; see Constant et al. (2017). Sag et al. (2002) refer to them as "a pain in the neck for NLP"; consequently their machine-supported recognition constitutes an ideal testbed for a variety of methodical approaches and is the subject of shared tasks; see, e.g., Markantonatou et al. (2020).

Fazly and Stevenson (2006) propose measures that quantify the degree of lexical and syntactic fixedness. Verma and Vuppuluri (2015) rely on lexical features in order to identify MWEs whose meanings differ from their components' meanings. Sporleder and Li (2009) include the collocational contexts of idiomatic MWEs into their computation; they model semantic relatedness with the help of lexical chains and cohesion graphs, and, based on this, compare supervised with unsupervised approaches for token-based idiom classification. Katz and Giesbrecht (2006) use latent semantic analysis in order to verify whether context word vector-similarity between idiomatic MWEs and its constituents helps with the calculation. Muzny and Zettlemoyer (2013) achieve a precision level of 65% for the distinction between idiomatic and literal wiktionary phrases, using lexical and graph-based features in order to quantify the assumption that literal phrases are more likely to have closely related words in their definition clause than idiomatic phrases. Salton et al. (2016) investigate whether Sentential Distributed Semantics of idiomatic verb-noun (VN) combinations show significant differences from non-idiomatic usage, and therefore train Sent2Vec models for sentence-level contexts. Using the same dataset, Peng et al. (2018) compute local context differences between word vector matrices on the basis of Frobenius norm. Senaldi et al. (2019) train vector-based models on a gold standard of VN constructions that has been annotated regarding idiomaticity on a 1-7 Likert scale. Hashempour and Villavicencio (2020) use contextualized word embeddings in order to distinguish between literal and idiomatic senses of MWEs that are treated as individual tokens in training and testing, producing average F1-scores of more than 70%.

We take up the idea of evaluating different context representations, expand corresponding measures with syntagmatic and other statistical features, and analyze how they complement each other to characterize idioms. Furthermore, we broaden the scope by extending the dataset beyond VN combinations, including all kinds of MWEs without morphosyntactic restrictions.

3 Dataset and features

The aim of this study is to evaluate quantitative features of MWEs with regard to their suitability of detecting idiomatic MWEs in a given text corpus. Contemporary pop song lyrics – a yet sparsely examined register – seem intrinsically promising for two reasons: Firstly, lyrics combine qualities of spoken and written language (Werner, 2012) with wordplay creativity (Kreyer, 2012) and can thus be expected to constitute a valuable source of both well-known and innovative idiomatic constructions. Secondly, on account of their formal structure, catchy and often idiomatic phrases tend to be repeated in choruses, so that there should be good prospects for empirical evidence. We use the freely available Corpus of German Song Lyrics (Schneider, 2020), covering a period of five decades and a broad range of artists, in order to ensure that our findings can be reproduced and compared by future studies. The general approach should also be applicable to languages other than German.

Although the corpus comes with XML-coded multi-layer annotations, we mainly work on the raw data and do not rely on linguistic preprocessing like parsing or lemmatization. To avoid reference to lexica or pre-defined syntactic template lists (like V-NP constructions), we include any ngram, spanning a minimum of two word tokens and a maximum of six word tokens within sentence boundaries. This yields a dataset of more than six million ngrams. From these we randomly select a sample of 10,000 ngrams.

This dataset is manually annotated by a native speaker in order to serve as a gold standard. To cope with the abovementioned fact that idiomatic status cannot always be described as either clearly idiomatic or clearly literal, we allow for three categories and mark idiom candidates as either literal, idiomatic, or partly idiomatic, where the latter comprises ngrams with both idiomatic and non-idiomatic content, which are excluded for our analysis, see Table 4 in Section 4, for exact numbers.

As a starting point for our evaluation, each dataset entry is automatically annotated with a number of features. We distinguish between three main groups of features to characterize idioms, for a detailed break down see Table 5.

Syntagmatic features (SY) measure collocation strength between all word pairs within an idiom candidate. Context features (CO) measure semantic similarity between the words within an idiom candidate and the words in its left/right context. Finally, other features (O) represent a variety of counts to assess the amount of evidence available, such as number of words in an idiom candidate.

SY_C1 and SY_C2 comprise a number of count-based collocation measures between a word and its neighbours within a window of +/- 5[1] (Evert, 2008). SY_C1 are based on the counts in DeReKo (Kupietz et al., 2010), whereas SY_C2 are based on the counts in the pop lyrics corpus. These count-based measures all aim at identifying MWEs that occur more often than randomly expected. We expect that idioms, like other MWEs, are characterized by high SY_C.

SY_W comprises a number of predictive collocation measures. These are all calculated by aggregating the output activations in a three layer neural network using the structured skipgram variant (Ling et al., 2015) of word2vec (Mikolov et al., 2013), again with a window size of +/- 5[2]. As shown by Levy and Goldberg (2014), these output activations approximate the shifted pointwise mutual information[3]. These predictive measures generalize from actually used collocations by means of dimensionality reduction in the hidden layer and thus can also predict unseen but meaningful collocations. However, due to generalization they are typically biased towards the dominant, usually literal usage. Thus, we expect that idioms, unlike other MWEs, are characterized by low SY_W.

Tables 1 and 2 exemplify the interplay between count-based and predictive collocations. Among the top 10 count-based collocates of 'Kuh' (cow), there are 6 collocates (in bold) stemming from idiomatic use, for example, 'die Kuh vom Eis kriegen' literally for 'getting the cow from the ice' meaning 'working out a situation'. In contrast, the predictive collocates all pertain to the literal meaning of cow as a domestic animal; e.g., 'Eis' does not occur among the top 400 predictive collocates.

The count-based and predictive collocates of 'Versuch' ('attempt'), on the other hand, show no such difference. Both refer to the literal meaning

Kuh	German	English
Count	Kalles **heilige blöde Blinde Bunte** lila Rosmarie **dumme** Yvonne **Eis**	Kalle's **holy silly blind colorful** purple Rosemary **stupid** Yvonne **ice**
Pred	ausgebüxte geschlachtete entlaufene geklonte trächtige geschlachteten weidende verwesende Kalles tote	escaped slaughtered runaway cloned pregnant slaughtered grazing decaying Kalle's dead

Table 1: Count-based and predictive collocates for Kuh (cow)

Versuch	German	English
Count	unternommen gescheitert Beim zweiten gescheiterten wert dritten gestartet unternehmen scheiterte	made failed in second failed worth third started make failed
Pred	untauglicher vergeblicher missglückter unternommene krampfhaften fehlgeschlagener (...)	unsuitable futile failed made convulsive failed failed desperate unsuitable desperate

Table 2: Count-based and predictive collocates for Versuch (attempt)

of 'Versuch'. However, also here we can observe a bias of the predictive collocates towards 'failed attempts'.

SY_R comprises non-parametric variants for some collocation measures by means of their ranks to account for the different scales of SY_C1 and SY_W. This includes SY_C1_R, SY_W_R1, SY_W_R2, and the rank difference SY_R_D.

As depicted in Equation 1, for all syntagmatic collocation measures *col*, we take the average over all pairs of words w_i, w_j in an idiom candidate of size $|w|$. Null-values, occurring when there exists no pair with measures from DeReKo, are transformed

---

[1] All measures with *autofocus* (AF) select those neighbours in the window which maximize the measure.

[2] DeReKoVecs (Fankhauser and Kupietz, 2019, http://corpora.ids-mannheim.de/openlab/derekovecs, accessed 2021-04-23)) has been trained on DeReKo.

[3] $SPMI(w, w_i) = log(\frac{p(w, w_i)}{p(w)p(w_i)}) - log(k)$, with k the number of negative samples used during training, and $p(w)$, $p(w_i)$, $p(w, w_i)$ the individual and joint relative frequencies of a word w and its neighbour w_i

Figure 1: Local context of ngrams

to min (or max) values appropriate for each feature.

$$\sum_{i \neq j} col(w_i, w_j) / |w|(|w| - 1) \tag{1}$$

The context features CO_VEC and CO_VEC_LEX aim at identifying idioms based on the heuristics that they occur within unusual thematic contexts. Idiomatic ngrams such as 'Perlen vor die Säue werfen' ('cast pearls before swine') are often found in local contexts that are thematically rather untypical for non-idiomatic uses of the individual ngram words. The expression can be expected in a theatre review or a political speech, but rather not in texts explicitly dealing with jewellery or livestock. To this end, CO_VEC uses cosine similarity between word vectors, which identifies paradigmatically related words occurring in similar usage contexts, comprising (near) synonyms, but also hyponyms, meronyms, etc.

Continuing with the above example, among the most similar words for 'Perle' are words like 'Kostbarkeit' ('preciousness'), 'Schatztruhe' ('treasure chest'), 'Liebeserklärung' ('declaration of love') or 'Brosche' ('brooch'). Close to 'Säue', we find 'Rindvieh' ('cattle'), 'Schafe' ('sheep'), 'Köter' ('pooch'), 'Hufe' ('hooves') or 'Schlachtbank' ('slaughterhouse'). Assuming that these words appear less likely in the local contexts of our example idiom than in the typical contexts of its constituents, low value for CO_VEC may indicate idiomatic use.

More specifically, CO_VEC is calculated as the mean cosine similarity between all pairs of words w_i in the idiom candidate of size $|w|$ and words c_j in the left/right context of size $|c|$ (in the present case we include five context words to the left and right[4]; see Figure 1 and Equation 2). CO_VEC_LEX is calculated like CO_VEC, but only takes lexical words into account, i.e. nouns, verbs, adverbs and adjectives. If the idiom candidate appears at several places within the corpus, an average is calculated.

$$\sum_{i,j} sim(w_i, c_j) / |w||c| \tag{2}$$

The last group O comprises O_GRAM, the number of words in an idiom candidate, O_NSTOPW[5], the number of non stopwords, and O_DEREKO, the number of words for which a word embedding is available.

In summary, the syntagmatic features (SY) analyze idiom candidates for frequent (SY_C), but unusual (SY_W) collocations along the syntagmatic axis to assess their phraseness and non transparency. The context features (CO) analyze their surrounding context for unsimilar words along the paradigmatic axis as a complementary measure of non transparency. Both feature sets utilize the observation that word embeddings are typically biased towards the dominant/transparent meaning.

4 Methods and results

To evaluate our feature set we have trained a Random Forest classifier [6]. Unless stated explicitly otherwise, all results have been obtained using 5-fold cross validation. To avoid overlap between training and test sets, we have removed all duplicates after lower-casing and stopword removal, leaving a dataset with 542 idioms and 8697 non-idioms.

Because this dataset is highly unbalanced, we have systematically varied the Random Forest's cutoff hyperparameter (default 0.5). As shown in Figure 2, a cutoff of 0.3 achieves the best F1-Score of 61.9%, balancing recall and precision around 62%. The best balanced accuracy of 83% is achieved at a much smaller cutoff of about 0.05. This may be a more appropriate cutoff for explorative idiom detection, where sensitivity (recall) is more important than precision.

To assess the contribution of the individual feature sets, we compare classification performance between using all features, each feature set individually, and subsets of features obtained by excluding individual feature sets.

Table 3 summarizes the results [7]: All individual feature sets except O contribute to classification performance. The biggest contribution comes from the collocation features based on DeReKo counts (SY_C1), followed by the collocation features based on the (much smaller) pop lyrics corpus (SY_C2) and the predictive collocation features SY_W.

---

[4]Similar measures, applied to context words within sentence boundaries, has been used in Köper and Schulte im Walde (2017) or Kurfalı and Östling (2020) for the detection of non-literal meaning.

[5]SY_C1 and S_W features are calculated on the idiom candidate after stopword removal.

[6]Support Vector Machines yield similar accuracies and scores.

[7]Standard deviation of Balanced Accuracy, measured over 10 5 x cross validations with different seeds is around 0.5 for all feature combinations.

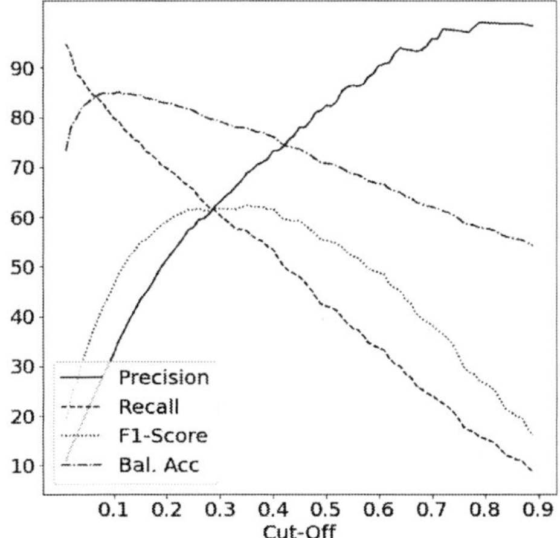

Figure 2: Trade-off curves for Random Forest cut-off

Feature set	Precision	Recall	F1-Score	Bal. Acc.
All features	62.7	59.9	61.3	78.9
SY_C1	44.2	38.7	41.2	67.8
SY_C2	32.9	30.6	31.7	63.4
SY_W	39.2	24.9	30.3	61.3
SY_R	31.2	28.0	29.5	62.1
CO	11.8	7.4	9.1	52.0
O	0.0	0.0	0.0	50.0
w/o SY_C1_R	55.8	48.9	52.1	73.2
w/o SY_C2	60.3	53.3	56.5	75.6
w/o SY_W_R	61.0	58.7	59.8	78.2
w/o SY_R	63.0	60.9	61.9	79.3
w/o CO	59.9	60.3	60.1	78.9
w/o O	61.0	55.9	58.3	76.8

Table 3: Performance of different feature sets in a Random Forest with cutoff=0.3. SY_C1: Count-based collocation measures based on DeReKo. SY_C2: Count-based collocation measures based on pop lyric corpus. SY_W: Predictive collocation measures. SY_R: Rank-based collocation measures. SY_C1_R: SY_C1+SY_R, SY_W_R: SY_W+SY_R. CO: Context features. O: Other

The bottom half of the table analyzes how much performance is lost when excluding a feature set. The relative order is largely consistent with the upper half. In particular, also from this perspective, count-based collocations SY_C1 (including their rank variants) turn out to be most important, i.e., they lead to the largest loss in performance.

Interestingly, omitting the other features (O) also decreases performance, even though they do not contribute individually. This may be due to the fact that they do not model intrinsic characteristics of idioms, but just the number of word pairs available for estimating SY and CO feature sets, i.e., essentially the amount of evidence available. Thus they are only useful in combination with other feature sets.

For SY_R the effect is the other way around. SY_R has a remarkable F1-Score of 29.5% when taken alone, but the overall performance increases, when the classifier is trained on all feature sets but SY_R. The lack of loss in performance may be due to the fact SY_R is highly correlated with SY_C1 and SY_W by construction, and thus does not add information. The slight increase seems to be a random effect.

Table 4 details the classification performance for the best feature set (w/o SY_R). Interestingly enough, when inspecting the false positives, we find that our approach identifies full idioms overlooked by the manual dataset annotation, such as 'in meine Fußstapfen treten' ('follow in my footsteps') or 'hinter Gitterstäben' (lit. 'behind thick bars', meaning: 'in prison'). We also see partly idiomatic MWEs like 'süßes Gift' ('sweet poison'), as well as supposedly incomplete idioms like 'nur ein leeres [Versprechen?]' ('only an empty [promise?]'). The automatic classification even detects previously hidden teenage slang idioms such as 'Optik schieben' (lit 'to push optics', approximately: 'to be under the influence of hallucinogenic drugs'). Besides, related phenomena like metaphors ('fahren in Richtung Gold', literal: 'drive towards gold') and allegories ('das ganze Leben ist ein Quiz', literal: 'all of life is a quiz') are labelled. Indeed, approximately 8% of the false positives show idiomatic or figurative use.

In order to better understand the interplay between features, Table 5 analyzes the contributions of the individual features for the classification task. *MDA* gives the random forest's estimate of the mean decrease in accuracy per feature, *IGain*

prediction outcome

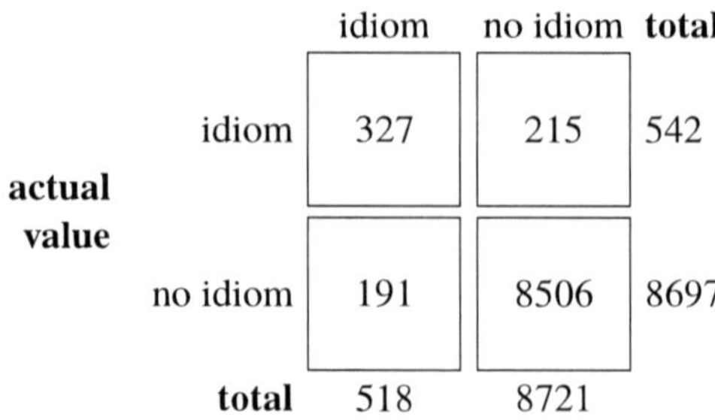

		idiom	no idiom	**total**
actual value	idiom	327	215	542
	no idiom	191	8506	8697
	total	518	8721	

Table 4: Confusion Matrix for prediction with the best feature set

the information gain (*1000), *TTest* the degree of significance by a Welch two sample t-test for confidence levels 0.95 (*), 0.99 (**), and 0.999 (***), and Δ the sign of the difference between the mean of a feature for idioms vs. non-idioms.

The context features CO_VEC and CO_VEC_LEX have the highest *MDA* followed by the other features O and the count-based collocation features estimated from the pop lyrics corpus SY_C2. All collocation (and rank) features estimated from DeReKo are in a similar range. Note however, that *MDA* tends to be shared among correlated features.

IGain assesses the individual (univariate) contribution of the features for classification. The two estimates of the overall frequency of an idiom candidate O_C2_N and O_C2_SGT have the highest *IGain*, closely followed by the count-based collocation features SY_C2 and SY_C1. The predictive collocation features SY_W and context features CO have slightly smaller *IGain*. This largely corroborates the results of the analysis of feature sets above.

With the exception of CO_VEC and two of the predictive collocation features, the difference between the means of all features in idioms vs. non-idioms is highly significant.

To better understand the contribution of the individual features, it is helpful to look at the difference Δ between their means: Compared to all non-idioms, words within idioms have a lower cosine similarity CO_VEC (but still higher CO_VEC_LEX) to their left and right neighbours, i.e., indeed they occur in unusual contexts. On the other hand, they have a higher count-based and predictive collocation strength among each other (SY_C1, SY_C2, SY_W) with some exceptions (SY_C1_LL,SY_W_CON,SY_W_NSUMAF).

Consequently, they also have a smaller rank for these measures (SY_C1_R, SY_W_R1, SY_W_R2), although we would expect larger ranks.

However, non-idioms comprise random ngrams that do not occur more often than expected as well as frequent MWEs with high collocation strength. Thus it is instructive to constrain the comparsion as follows: Δ' gives the sign of the difference between the mean for idioms and all those non-idioms with SY_C1_LD larger than the mean of SY_C1_LD of all non-idioms, i.e., only the non-idiomatic but still frequent MWEs. Incidentally, all these differences are highly significant (at least 0.99), with the exception of CO_VEC. In this comparison, the context features CO and both, the count-based and predictive collocation features estimated from DeReKo (SY_C1 and SY_W, except SY_C1_MI,) are smaller, and accordingly the corresponding rank features are larger for idioms. In particular, the rank difference SY_R_D between count-based and predictive collocation is larger, i.e., co-occuring words in an idiom tend to be less represented by the predictive collocations which are biased towards the dominant meaning.

In summary, idioms, like non-idiomatic MWEs, are characterized by high collocation strength in comparison to randomly selected ngrams. However, in comparison with non-idiomatic but frequent MWEs, they are characterized by occurring in unusual contexts (low CO_VEC), and by low predictive collocation strength SY_W; or, put more bluntly, idiomatic MWEs occur frequently but are unusual.

To demonstrate the transferability of our approach, we have applied it to a dataset of German idioms extracted from German Wikipedia[8]. After removing duplicates (72) with our gold standard [9], and all idioms that consist of less than 2 words after stopword removal, this set comprises 760 idioms.

As training set for this out-of-domain scenario, we use a sample of 80% of non-idioms and all idioms of our base data set. The test set consists of the remaining 20% of the non-idioms and the Wikipedia idioms. We train the classifier on the feature ensemble SY_C1 + SY_W + SY_R + O (without the feature O_DEREKO). This is because the feature sets SY_C2 and CO are calculated based on

---

[8]https://de.wikipedia.org/wiki/ Liste_deutscher_Redewendungen, accessed February, 22, 2021.

[9]All these duplicates have been independently annotated correctly as idioms.

Feature	MDA	IGain	TTest	Δ	Δ′	Description
SY_C1_LD	9.8	30.4	***	+	-	logdice (Rychlý, 2008)
SY_C1_LDAF	11.7	34.3	***	+	-	logdice with autofocus
SY_C1_LL	13.7	43.4	***	-	-	loglikelihood
SY_C1_MI	19.5	48.5	***	+	+	(pointwise) mutual information, MI
SY_C1_MI3	11.7	34.8	***	+	-	MI³ (Daille, 1994)
SY_C2_LD	20.3	19.4	***	+	+	logdice in pop lyrics corpus
SY_C2_LL	12.1	51.8	***	+	+	loglikelihood in pop lyrics corpus
SY_C2_MI	13.6	52.8	***	+	+	(pointwise) mutual information, MI in pop lyrics corpus
SY_C2_MI3	11.8	51.2	***	+	+	MI³ in pop lyrics corpus
SY_C2_G	23.5	12.4	***	+	+	lexical gravity in pop lyrics corpus (Daudaravičius and Marcinkevičienė, 2004; Gries and Mukherjee, 2010)
SY_C2_N	10.7	49.6	***	+	+	number of occurrences in pop lyrics corpus
SY_C2_SGT	19.0	55.2	***	+	+	Simple Good-Turing estimate of probability in pop lyrics corpus
SY_W_AVG	12.7	19.0	*	+	-	average of output activations with autofocus
SY_W_CON	13.9	20.5	***	-	-	conorm of column normalized output activations with autofocus
SY_W_MAX	10.2	11.6	***	+	-	max of output activations
SY_W_NSUM	10.6	16.7		+	-	sum of output activations normalized by total sum over all columns
SY_W_NSUMAF	20.2	30.1		-	-	sum of output activations normalized by total sum over all selected columns with autofocus
SY_C1_R	16.9	53.0	***	-	+	rank by SY_C_LD
SY_W_R1	14.3	23.0	***	-	+	rank by SY_W_CON
SY_W_R2	13.9	20.5	***	-	+	rank by SY_W_NSUM
SY_R_D	18.9	55.0	***	+	+	rank difference: SY_W_R1-SY_C1_R
CO_VEC	24.3	14.4		-	-	avg. cosine similarity between words in ngram and words in +/-5 context in pop lyrics corpus
CO_VEC_LEX	20.8	13.9	*	+	-	like CO_WIN5_VEC but only on lexical words
O_GRAM	17.2	13.5	***	-	-	number of ngram words
O_DEREKO	15.1	12.3		-	-	number of ngram words available in DeReKo
O_NSTOPW	29.6	14.7	***	-	-	number of non stop words in ngram

Table 5: Features

5   Conclusions

The aim of this study was to model well-studied idiom characteristics with quantitative features and to evaluate them on suitable datasets. Our evaluations show that count-based collocation measures indeed characterize idioms' frequent usage and stable occurrence, i.e. phraseness. The predictive collocation measures and the context features on the other hand are able to model uncommon usage, that is, non transparency.

By applying our model, trained on an annotated dataset that was sampled from a pop lyrics corpus, to an out-of-domain dataset of idioms crawled from Wikipedia, we demonstrated the generalizability of our approach.

The introduced features do not require sophisticated or knowledge intensive preprocessing, and need only minimal context. Even, when no context is available, as for the out-of-domain dataset, we achieve state-of-the art classification performance.

However, the feature set also has limitations. For idioms that consist of only one content word, possibly with some stopwords, the collocation measures do not produce very meaningful results. In this case we need to entirely rely on the context features. In a similar vein, count based collocation strength obviously does not apply to novel idioms. Moreover, when idiomatic use constitutes the overwhelmingly dominant use, such as 'kenne meine Pappenheimer' (literal: 'know my Pappenheimers', roughly: 'know the weak people (in my team)'), neither CO nor SY_W features can contribute.

But in sum, all evaluation results – and the detailed analysis of how the count-based and predictive features complement each other for discriminating between idioms and non idioms – shed an additional empirical light on the linguistically intricate and multifaceted phenomenon of idiomaticity. Waiving limitations on morphosyntactic templates (like, e.g., VN constructions), our approach should work well for any potentially idiomatic MWEs.

For future work, we intend to apply the approach to bigger datasets; attractive candidates might be the corpora of the PARSEME (PARsing and Multiword Expressions) network Savary et al. (2018) or the COLF-VID dataset of verbal idioms Ehren et al. (2020). We will also experiment with additional features, in particular to better capture fixedness of idiomaticity and cope with non transparent compound idiomatic words.

All data and source code is publicly available

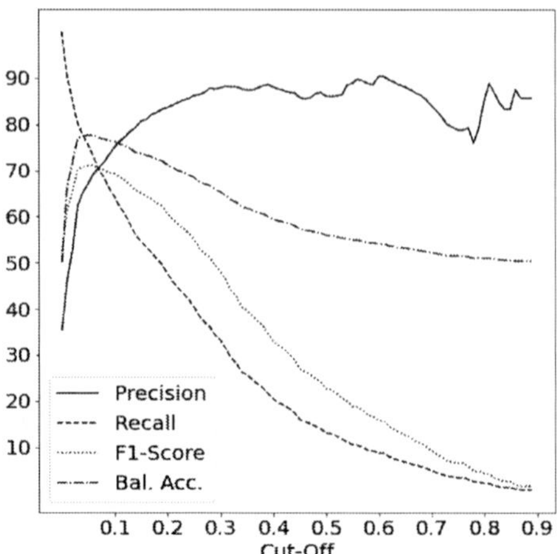

Figure 3: Trade-off curves for Random Forest cut-off on the Wikipedia dataset

prediction outcome

		idiom	no idiom	**total**
	idiom	528	232	760
actual value				
	no idiom	247	1135	1382
	total	775	1367	

Table 6: Confusion Matrix for prediction on idioms from Wikipedia with cut-off=0.05

the ngram context within the pop lyrics corpus and are consequently not available for out-of-domain data. Figure 3 shows the trade-off curves of the predictions on the Wikipedia dataset for a range of cut-off thresholds.

The obtained results are rather convincing. With a cutoff threshold of 0.05, the classifier achieves an F1-Score of 71.0% and a recall of 80.3%, which means that the classifier is able to detect the majority of the unknown Wikipedia idioms. While not directly comparable due to different datasets and classification tasks, these results are in the same ballpark as e.g. Hashempour and Villavicencio (2020) who report F1-Scores of 70%.

Table 6 gives the confusion matrix of the prediction on the unknown idioms.

under a Creative Commons license at `http://songkorpus.de/data/`.

References

Timothy Baldwin and Su Nam Kim. 2010. Multiword expressions. In Nitin Indurkhya and Fred J. Damerau, editors, *Handbook of Natural Language Processing, Second Edition*, pages 267–292. CRC Press, Boca Raton.

Mathieu Constant, Gülşen Eryiğit, Johanna Monti, Lonneke van der Plas, Carlos Ramisch, Michael Rosner, and Amalia Todirascu. 2017. Survey: Multiword expression processing: A Survey. *Computational Linguistics*, 43(4):837–892.

Béatrice Daille. 1994. *Approche mixte pour l'extraction de terminologie: statistique lexicale et filtres linguistiques*. Ph.D. thesis, Paris 7.

Vidas Daudaravičius and Rūta Marcinkevičienė. 2004. Gravity counts for the boundaries of collocations. *International Journal of Corpus Linguistics*, 9(2):321–348.

Rafael Ehren, Timm Lichte, Laura Kallmeyer, and Jakub Waszczuk. 2020. Supervised disambiguation of German verbal idioms with a BiLSTM architecture. In *Proceedings of the Second Workshop on Figurative Language Processing*, Online. Association for Computational Linguistics.

Stefan Evert. 2008. Corpora and collocations. In Anke Lüdeling and Merja Kytö, editors, *Corpus Linguistics. An International Handbook*, chapter 58, pages 1212–1248. Mouton de Gruyter, Berlin, Germany.

Peter Fankhauser and Marc Kupietz. 2019. Analyzing domain specific word embeddings for a large corpus of contemporary German. In *International Corpus Linguistics Conference, Cardiff, Wales, UK, July 22-26, 2019*, Mannheim. Leibniz-Institut für Deutsche Sprache (IDS).

Afsaneh Fazly and Suzanne Stevenson. 2006. Automatically constructing a lexicon of verb phrase idiomatic combinations. In *Proceedings of the 11st Conference of the European Chapter of the Association for Computational Linguistics (EACL)*, pages 337–344.

Dafydd Gibbon. 1982. Violations of frege's principle and their significance for contrastive semantics. *Papers and Studies in Contrastive Linguistics*, 14:5–24.

Stefan Gries. 2008. Phraseology and linguistic theory: A brief survey. In Sylviane Granger and Fanny Meunier, editors, *Phraseology: An interdisciplinary perspective*, pages 3–25. Amsterdam: John Benjamins.

Stefan Gries and Joybrato Mukherjee. 2010. Lexical gravity across varieties of english: An ice-based study of n-grams in asian englishes. *International Journal of Corpus Linguistics*, 15:520–548.

Reyhaneh Hashempour and Aline Villavicencio. 2020. Leveraging contextual embeddings and idiom principle for detecting idiomaticity in potentially idiomatic expressions. In *Proceedings of the Workshop on the Cognitive Aspects of the Lexicon*, pages 72–80. Association for Computational Linguistics.

Graham Katz and Eugenie Giesbrecht. 2006. Automatic identification of non-compositional multiword expressions using latent semantic analysis. In *Proceedings of the Workshop on Multiword Expressions: Identifying and Exploiting Underlying Properties*, pages 12–19, Sydney, Australia. Association for Computational Linguistics.

Rolf Kreyer. 2012. "Love is like a stove – it burns you when it's hot": A corpus-linguistic view on the (non-)creative use of love-related metaphors in pop songs. *Language and Computers*, pages 103–115.

Marc Kupietz, Cyril Belica, Holger Keibel, and Andreas Witt. 2010. The German Reference Corpus DeReKo: A Primordial Sample for Linguistic Research. In *Proceedings of the Seventh International Conference On Language Resources And Evaluation (LREC'10)*, page 1848–1854, Valletta / Paris. European Language Resources Association (ELRA).

Murathan Kurfalı and Robert Östling. 2020. Disambiguation of potentially idiomatic expressions with contextual embeddings. In *Proceedings of the Joint Workshop on Multiword Expressions and Electronic Lexicons*, pages 85–94, online. Association for Computational Linguistics.

Maximilian Köper and Sabine Schulte im Walde. 2017. Applying multi-sense embeddings for German verbs to determine semantic relatedness and to detect non-literal language. In *Proceedings of the 15th Conference of the European Chapter of the Association for Computational Linguistics: Volume 2, Short Papers*, pages 535–542.

Omer Levy and Yoav Goldberg. 2014. Neural word embedding as implicit matrix factorization. In *Advances in Neural Information Processing Systems (NIPS)*.

Wang Ling, Chris Dyer, Alan W. Black, and Isabel Trancoso. 2015. Two/too simple adaptations of Word2Vec for syntax problems. In *Proceedings of the 2015 Conference of the North American Chapter of the Association for Computational Linguistics: Human Language Technologies*, pages 1299–1304, Denver, Colorado. Association for Computational Linguistics.

Stella Markantonatou, John McCrae, Jelena Mitrović, Carole Tiberius, Carlos Ramisch, Ashwini Vaidya, Petya Osenova, and Agata Savary, editors. 2020. *Proceedings of the Joint Workshop on Multiword Expressions and Electronic Lexicons*. Association for Computational Linguistics.

Tomas Mikolov, Ilya Sutskever, Kai Chen, Greg S Corrado, and Jeff Dean. 2013. Distributed representations of words and phrases and their compositionality. In *Advances in Neural Information Processing Systems*, volume 26. Curran Associates, Inc.

Grace Muzny and Luke Zettlemoyer. 2013. Automatic idiom identification in Wiktionary. In *Proceedings of the 2013 Conference on Empirical Methods in Natural Language Processing*, pages 1417–1421, Seattle, Washington, USA. Association for Computational Linguistics.

Jing Peng, Katsiaryna Aharodnik, and Anna Feldman. 2018. A distributional semantics model for idiom detection - the case of english and russian. *ICAART*, pages 675–682.

Manali Pradhan, Jing Peng, Anna Feldman, and Bianca Wright. 2018. Idioms: Humans or machines, it's all about context. In *Computational Linguistics and Intelligent Text Processing - 18th International Conference, CICLing 2017, Revised Selected Papers*, Lecture Notes in Computer Science (including subseries Lecture Notes in Artificial Intelligence and Lecture Notes in Bioinformatics), pages 291–304. Springer.

Pavel Rychlý. 2008. A lexicographer-friendly association score. *Proceedings of the 2nd Workshop on Recent Advances in Slavonic Natural Languages Processing, RASLAN*, pages 6–9.

Ivan A. Sag, Timothy Baldwin, Francis Bond, Ann Copestake, and Dan Flickinger. 2002. Multiword expressions: A pain in the neck for nlp. In *Computational Linguistics and Intelligent Text Processing*, pages 1–15, Berlin, Heidelberg. Springer Berlin Heidelberg.

Giancarlo Salton, John Kelleher, and Robert Ross. 2016. Idiom token classification using sentential distributed semantics. In *Proceedings of the 54th Annual Meeting of the Association for Computational Linguistics (Volume 1: Long Papers)*, pages 194–204.

Agata Savary, Marie Candito, Verginica Mititelu, Eduard Bejček, Fabienne Cap, Slavomír Čéplö, Silvio Cordeiro, Gülşen Eryiğit, Voula Giouli, Maarten Van Gompel, Yaakov HaCohen-Kerner, Jolanta Kovalevskaitė, Simon Krek, Chaya Liebeskind, Johanna Monti, Carla Parra Escartín, Lonneke Der, Behrang Qasemi Zadeh, Carlos Ramisch, and Veronika Vincze. 2018. Parseme multilingual corpus of verbal multiword expressions. In Stella Markantonatou, Carlos Ramisch, Agata Savary, and Veronika Vincze, editors, *Multiword expressions at length and in depth: Extended papers from the MWE 2017 workshop*, pages 87–147.

Nathan Schneider, Emily Danchik, Chris Dyer, and Noah Smith. 2014. Discriminative lexical semantic segmentation with gaps: Running the mwe gamut. *Transactions of the Association for Computational Linguistics*, 2:193–206.

Roman Schneider. 2020. A corpus linguistic perspective on contemporary german pop lyrics with the multi-layer annotated "songkorpus". In *Proceedings of The 12th Language Resources and Evaluation Conference, LREC 2020, Marseille, France, May 11-16, 2020*, pages 842–848. European Language Resources Association.

Marco S. G. Senaldi, Yuri Bizzoni, and A. Lenci. 2019. What do neural networks actually learn, when they learn to identify idioms? In *Proceedings of the Society for Computation in Linguistics (SCiL)*, volume 2, pages 310–313.

John Sinclair. 1991. *Corpus, concordance, collocation*. University Press, Oxford.

Caroline Sporleder and Linlin Li. 2009. Unsupervised recognition of literal and non-literal use of idiomatic expressions. In *Proceedings of the 12th Conference of the European Chapter of the ACL (EACL 2009)*, pages 754–762.

Anatol Stefanowitsch and Stefan Th. Gries, editors. 2007. *Corpus-Based Approaches to Metaphor and Metonymy*. De Gruyter Mouton.

Rakesh Verma and Vasanthi Vuppuluri. 2015. A new approach for idiom identification using meanings and the web. In *Proceedings of Recent Advances in Natural Language Processing*, pages 681–687, Hissar, Bulgaria.

Valentin Werner. 2012. Love is all around: A corpus-based study of pop lyrics. *Corpora*, 7:19–50.

Stefanie Wulff. 2008. *Rethinking Idiomaticity: A Usage-based Approach*. Studies in Corpus and Discourse. Continuum, London, New York.

Contextualized Embeddings Encode Monolingual and Cross-lingual Knowledge of Idiomaticity

Samin Fakharian and **Paul Cook**
Faculty of Computer Science, University of New Brunswick
Fredericton, NB E3B 5A3 Canada
{samin.fakharian,paul.cook}@unb.ca

Abstract

Potentially idiomatic expressions (PIEs) are ambiguous between non-compositional idiomatic interpretations and transparent literal interpretations. For example, *hit the road* can have an idiomatic meaning corresponding to 'start a journey' or have a literal interpretation. In this paper we propose a supervised model based on contextualized embeddings for predicting whether usages of PIEs are idiomatic or literal. We consider monolingual experiments for English and Russian, and show that the proposed model outperforms previous approaches, including in the case that the model is tested on instances of PIE types that were not observed during training. We then consider cross-lingual experiments in which the model is trained on PIE instances in one language, English or Russian, and tested on the other language. We find that the model outperforms baselines in this setting. These findings suggest that contextualized embeddings are able to learn representations that encode knowledge of idiomaticity that is not restricted to specific expressions, nor to a specific language.

1 Introduction

Multiword expressions (MWEs) are lexicalized combinations of multiple words, which display some form of idiomaticity (Baldwin and Kim, 2010). In this paper we focus on potentially-idiomatic expressions (PIEs), i.e., expressions which are ambiguous between a semantically-opaque idiomatic interpretation, and a compositional literal meaning. In the following example, the English PIE *hit the road* has an idiomatic meaning corresponding roughly to 'start a journey':

1. The marchers had <u>hit the road</u> before 0500 hours and by midday they were limping back having achieved success on day one.

On the other hand, *hit the road*, can also be used literally, as in the example below:

2. Two climbers dislodged another huge block which <u>hit the road</u> within 18 inches of one of the estate's senior guides.[1]

PIEs occur across languages, with one particularly common class of PIE cross-lingually being verb–noun combinations (VNCs, Fazly et al., 2009) — i.e., PIEs consisting of a verb with a noun in its direct object position — such as *hit the road* in the example above. Although VNCs are common, PIEs also occur in other syntactic constructions, with English examples including combinations of a verb and prepositional phrase — e.g., *skating on thin ice* (which can be used idiomatically to mean roughly 'at risk') — and prepositional phrases — e.g., *off the hook* (with a potential idiomatic meaning of roughly 'out of danger'). Distinguishing between literal and idiomatic usages of PIEs could be particularly important for down-stream natural language processing applications such as machine translation (Isabelle et al., 2017).

Previous work has considered both unsupervised and supervised approaches to predicting the token-level idiomaticity of PIEs. However, annotated data to train supervised approaches is not available for all PIEs in all languages. This makes unsupervised approaches (e.g., Fazly et al., 2009; Haagsma et al., 2018; Liu and Hwa, 2018; Kurfalı and Östling, 2020), which do not have this resource requirement, appealing. On the other hand, supervised approaches (e.g., Salton et al., 2016; King and Cook, 2018) tend to outperform unsupervised approaches, but are restricted to languages and PIEs for which annotated training data is available.

In this paper we consider supervised approaches based on contextualized embeddings (Devlin et al., 2019; Liu et al., 2019; Kuratov and Arkhipov, 2019) to predicting usages of PIEs as idiomatic

---

[1]These example sentences are taken, with light editing, from the VNC-Tokens dataset (Cook et al., 2008).

Proceedings of the 17th Workshop on Multiword Expressions, pages 23–32
Bangkok, Thailand (online), August 6, 2021. ©2021 Association for Computational Linguistics

or literal; however, we measure the ability of these approaches to generalize to expressions that were not observed during training, and also to generalize across languages. We begin by considering monolingual experiments for English and Russian in which we train and test on instances of the same PIEs. For English, we focus on VNCs (Cook et al., 2008). For Russian, we consider a wider-range of types of PIEs (Aharodnik et al., 2018). We then consider a second monolingual setting in which we evaluate on PIEs, again either English or Russian, that were not observed during training. Finally, we consider cross-lingual detection of idiomaticity. Here we train on instances of PIEs in one language, English or Russian, and evaluate on instances of PIEs in the other language.

Our findings evaluating on expressions that were observed during training are similar to those of (Kurfalı and Östling, 2020); we achieve strong improvements over baselines, and on English outperform previous approaches based on conventional word embeddings (King and Cook, 2018). In monolingual experiments evaluating on PIEs that were not observed during training, we again improve over baselines, and in the case of English, also over a strong linguistically-informed unsupervised baseline. In cross-lingual experiments, in which the model is evaluated on instances of PIEs in a language that was not observed during training, we again improve over baselines, and remarkably observe performance roughly on par with that of monolingual experiments evaluating on expressions not observed during training. These findings suggest that contextualized embeddings are able to learn representations that encode knowledge of idiomaticity that is not restricted to specific expressions, nor to a specific language.

2 Related Work

Previous work has considered unsupervised and supervised approaches to predicting the token-level idiomaticity of PIEs. Although unsupervised methods have been proposed to disambiguate a wide range of kinds of potentially-idiomatic expressions (Haagsma et al., 2018; Liu and Hwa, 2018; Kurfalı and Östling, 2020), and are not limited to languages and types of PIEs for which training data is available, these approaches tend to not perform as well as supervised approaches.

Focusing on specific languages and types of expressions can improve unsupervised approaches.

For example, focusing on VNCs, the idiomatic interpretations of VNCs are typically lexico-syntactically fixed. Returning to the *hit the road* example from Section 1, the idiomatic interpretation is typically not accessible if the determiner is indefinite (e.g., *hit a road*), the noun is plural (e.g., *hit the roads*), or the voice is passive (e.g., *the road was hit*); in such cases typically only the literal interpretation is available. Fazly et al. (2009) propose an unsupervised statistical method based on the lexico-syntactic fixedness of VNCs to determine the canonical forms — with respect to the determiner, number of the noun, and voice of the verb — of VNCs. They observe that idiomatic usages of VNCs tend to occur in canonical forms, and that literal usages tend to occur in non-canonical forms. A strong, linguistically-informed unsupervised baseline for distinguishing literal from idiomatic VNC usages is therefore to label canonical form usages as idiomatic, and non-canonical form usages as literal.

Salton et al. (2016) propose a supervised approach to predicting the token-level idiomaticity of PIEs, focusing on English VNCs, based on training an SVM on skip-thoughts (Kiros et al., 2015) representations of sentences containing PIEs. King and Cook (2018) achieve better results using a simpler sentence representation based on average of word embeddings. Moreover, King and Cook show that adding a single binary feature to the sentence representation indicating whether the VNC occurs in a canonical form — based on the method of Fazly et al. (2009) — gives substantial improvements. Hashempour and Villavicencio (2020) propose a supervised approach in which PIE instances are treated as single units by fusing their lexicalized component words, and learning representations of these units using word and contextualized (Melamud et al., 2016; Devlin et al., 2019) embeddings. Hashempour and Villavicencio also focus on VNCs. Although they show improvements by treating VNC instances as fused units, they do not outperform King and Cook; they do, however, train their models on smaller corpora. Shwartz and Dagan (2019) use representations of spans of tokens based on contextualized embedding for predicting a range of MWE properties. Most closely related to our work, they consider light-verb construction and verb-particle construction classification, for both of which there is an ambiguity between MWE usages and similar-on-the-surface literal combinations. Shwartz and Dagan do not, however, consider English VNCs or Russian idioms as we do.

Kurfalı and Östling (2020) propose a supervised approach to classifying instances of potentially-idiomatic expressions, as idiomatic or literal, based on contextualized embeddings. They represent MWE instances as the average of the contextual embeddings for the tokenized pieces of their lexicalized component words, which are lemmatized in a preprocessing step, and use a single-layer perceptron for classification. Their findings indicate that their approach improves over previous approaches on English and German PIEs. In this paper, similarly to Kurfalı and Östling, we consider an approach based on contextualized embeddings, but we consider experimental setups in which classifiers are evaluated on expressions, and also languages, that are unobserved during training.

3   Predicting PIE Idiomaticity with Contextualized Embeddings

Previous supervised approaches to identifying idiomatic instances of PIEs have represented PIE instances with sentence embeddings (Salton et al., 2016; King and Cook, 2018). We consider a similar approach here using contextualized embeddings from BERT (Devlin et al., 2019), RoBERTa (Liu et al., 2019), RuBERT (Kuratov and Arkhipov, 2019), and mBERT (Devlin et al., 2019). Specifically we represent a PIE instance using the CLS (classification) token for the context in which it occurs.[2] For representing English PIEs we use the sentence in which the target expression occurs as the context. For representing Russian PIEs, the dataset we use (discussed in Section 4.1) does not include sentence segmentation, and so we instead use a context of up to 300 characters to the left and right of the target expression.[3]

Because we focus on VNCs for English experiments, following King and Cook (2018), for our monolingual experiments on English VNCs, we also consider whether incorporating informa-

tion about lexico-syntactic fixedness of VNCs into our approach gives improvements. Specifically, we concatenate a single binary feature indicating whether a VNC usage is in a canonical form, referred to as CF, with the representation of the CLS token.

We fine tune pre-trained BERT, RoBERTa, RuBERT, and mBERT models for binary classification of PIE token instances as idiomatic or literal. We use two fully-connected layers on top of the contextualized embedding model. The first layer has the same dimensionality as the representation of the VNC (i.e., 768 dimensions, the hidden layer size of each of the contextualized embedding models considered, and an additional dimension when the CF feature is used) and uses the ReLU activation function. The second layer has 512 dimensions and uses the softmax activation function.

4   Materials and Methods

In this section we describe our datasets (Section 4.1), experimental setups and evaluation metric (Section 4.2), and then the implementation of our models and the parameter settings used (Section 4.3).

4.1   Datasets

Following Salton et al. (2016), King and Cook (2018), and Hashempour and Villavicencio (2020), for English, we use the VNC-Tokens dataset (Cook et al., 2008), which consists of English VNC usages extracted from the British National Corpus (Burnard, 2000) annotated as literal or idiomatic.[4] VNC-Tokens includes DEV (development) and TEST sets — referred to here as EN-DEV and EN-TEST to distinguish them from the Russian dataset introduced below — which each include roughly 600 instances of 14 VNC types. The expressions in EN-DEV and EN-TEST do not overlap. Each of EN-DEV and EN-TEST is roughly balanced with respect to idiomatic and literal instances. We use EN-DEV for hyper-parameter tuning, and carry out no such tuning on EN-TEST.

For Russian, we use the dataset of Aharodnik et al. (2018) which consists of instances of Russian PIEs annotated at the token level as literal or idiomatic. Unlike the English dataset, this dataset is not restricted to VNCs. It includes id-

---

[2]In preliminary experiments we also considered representations of English VNC instances formed by averaging and concatenating contextualized representations of the verb and noun components of a target VNC (where the verb and noun representations are themselves averages of the representations of the word pieces they are segmented into). We found these approaches to perform roughly on par with representing VNC instances using the CLS token, and so only consider this approach here.

[3]We did not attempt to tune this context window size, although there is scope to do so in future work.

[4]Following Salton et al. (2016), King and Cook (2018), and Hashempour and Villavicencio (2020), we ignore instances labelled as unknown in VNC-Tokens.

Dataset	# expressions	# tokens	% idiomatic
EN-DEV	14	594	60.9
EN-TEST	14	613	63.3
RUSSIAN	37	775	54.3

Table 1: The number of PIE types and tokens, and the percentage of idiomatic tokens, in each dataset.

ioms with a range of syntactic constructions including preposition+noun, preposition+adj+noun, and VNCs. The dataset consists of three sections containing classical prose, modern prose, and text from Russian Wikipedia. We consider only the Russian Wikipedia portion because classical prose is substantially older than the text in the English VNC-Tokens dataset (which is from the British National corpus, which primarily includes texts from the late twentieth century), and the modern prose portion is relatively small compared to the Russian Wikipedia portion, which includes roughly 500M tokens. Each instance is accompanied by a context window of up to three paragraphs. Meta-data for this dataset indicating the location of the target expression in the context unfortunately does not appear to be available. We therefore restrict our experiments to the subset of this dataset for which there is an exact match between the target expression and a token sequence in the context. This gives a dataset consisting of 37 expressions and 775 token instances.[5] The dataset is again roughly balanced between idiomatic and literal usages with 54.3% being idiomatic. In contrast to the English dataset, we do not split this Russian dataset at the type level into separate DEV and TEST datasets because we carry out no hyper-parameter tuning on this dataset. We refer to this dataset as RUSSIAN.

Statistics for the number of PIE types and tokens, and the percentage of idiomatic tokens, in each dataset, are given in Table 1.

4.2 Experimental Setups and Evaluation

We first consider an experimental setup similar to King and Cook (2018) and Kurfalı and Östling (2020), referred to here as "all expressions". In this monolingual experimental setup we train and test on instances of the same PIEs in the same language. For each of EN-DEV, EN-TEST, and RUSSIAN, we randomly partition the instances into

training (roughly 75%) and testing (roughly 25%) sets, keeping the ratio of idiomatic to literal usages of each expression balanced across the training and testing sets. We repeat this random partitioning 10 times. For EN-DEV and EN-TEST we use the same partitions as King and Cook.

We do not expect to have annotated instances of all PIE types, limiting the applicability of models developed for the all expressions experimental setup. We are therefore particularly interested in determining whether a supervised model is able to generalize to expressions that were unseen during training. Here we consider a second monolingual experimental setup proposed by Gharbieh et al. (2016), referred to here as "unseen expressions". In these experiments we hold out all instances of one PIE type for testing, and train on all instances of the remaining types (within either EN-DEV, EN-TEST, or RUSSIAN). We repeat this fourteen times for each of EN-DEV and EN-TEST, and 37 times for RUSSIAN, holding out each PIE type once for testing.

For both experimental setups — i.e., all expressions and unseen expressions — we train and test models on EN-DEV for preliminary experiments and setting parameters. We then report final results by training and testing models on EN-TEST and RUSSIAN.

Just as we do not expect to have annotated instances of all PIE types for a given language, we also do not expect to have annotated instances of PIEs for all languages. We therefore consider an extension of the monolingual unseen expressions experimental setup in which we evaluate on instances of PIEs in a language that was not observed during training, referred to as "cross-lingual". In these experiments we train on either English or Russian, and evaluate on the other language. In particular, we train on either EN-DEV or EN-TEST and evaluate on RUSSIAN, and also train on RUSSIAN and evaluate on each of EN-DEV and EN-TEST.

The idiomatic and literal classes for both the English and Russian datasets are roughly balanced (Table 1). We therefore evaluate using accuracy. For the all expressions experimental setup, we report average accuracy across the 10 runs. In the unseen expressions experimental setup, we repeatedly hold out each expression until all instances of each expression (within either EN-DEV, EN-TEST, or RUSSIAN) have been classified, and then compute accuracy. For the cross-lingual experiments,

---

[5]The entire Russian Wikipedia portion of the dataset consists of 40 expressions and 799 token instances. Restricting the dataset to instances that have an exact match with the target expression therefore still retains the majority of the data.

we simply calculate accuracy over all instances in the dataset used for testing.

4.3 Implementation and Parameter Settings

We use Huggingface (Wolf et al., 2020) implementations of BERT, RoBERTa, mBERT, and RuBERT. Specifically we use bert-base-uncased, roberta-base, bert-base-multilingual-cased, and rubert-base-cased. All models have 12 layers and a hidden layer size of 768. The number of parameters for BERT, RoBERTa, mBERT, and RuBERT, is 125M, 125M, 179M, and 180M, respectively. BERT and RoBERTa are trained on uncased and cased English text, respectively. mBERT is trained on text from 104 languages. RuBERT is trained on Russian Wikipedia and Russian news data. We use BERT, RoBERTa, and mBERT for monolingual English experiments; RuBERT and mBERT for monolingual Russian experiments; and mBERT for cross-lingual experiments.

We train our models using Adam optimizer (Kingma and Ba, 2015) to minimize the cross-entropy loss. We use the default dropout of 0.5 for the network layers which are on top of BERT, RoBERTa, mBERT, or RuBERT. For fine-tuning, Devlin et al. (2019) recommend the following parameter settings: batch size of 8, 16, or 32; epochs between 2 and 4; and learning rate of 2e-5, 3e-5, or 5e-5.

We perform grid search over these parameter settings on EN-DEV for the monolingual all expressions and unseen expressions experimental setups. We report results for the best parameter settings on EN-DEV, and then use only these parameter settings for experiments on EN-TEST and RUSSIAN. For the cross-lingual experiments, we do no further parameter tuning, and report results for the best parameter settings for the unseen expressions experimental setup for EN-DEV. We repeat the experiments 10 times with different random seeds, and report the mean accuracy and standard deviation over the runs.

5 Monolingual Results

In this section, we present results for the unseen and all expressions experimental setups, for monolingual experiments on English (Section 5.1) and Russian (Section 5.2). In Section 6 we present results for cross-lingual experiments.

5.1 English

For English, we compare against three baselines: a most-frequent class (MFC) baseline, the unsupervised approach of Fazly et al. (2009, CForm) based on canonical forms, and the supervised approach of King and Cook (2018).

We begin by considering results for the all expressions experimental setup. Results are shown in the top panel of Table 2 (labelled "All"). On each dataset, both BERT and RoBERTa outperform all baselines, including King and Cook (2018) when using the canonical form (CF) feature (indicated by "+CF" in Table 2). This finding demonstrates that contextualized embeddings are able to better capture knowledge of the idiomaticity of PIEs than previous approaches. mBERT performs relatively poorly compared to BERT and RoBERTa, although it still outperforms the baselines, with the exception of King and Cook when using the CF feature.

We now examine the impact of the CF feature in the all expressions experimental setup.[6] For each model based on contextualized embeddings, incorporating the CF feature gives an improvement, but these improvements are small relative to the standard deviation across runs. This is in contrast to the substantial improvements obtained by King and Cook (2018) when using the CF feature. These findings suggest that contextualized embeddings are able to better capture the linguistic knowledge encoded in this feature than conventional word embeddings, which King and Cook use to represent VNC instances.

We now consider results for the unseen expressions experimental setup. Results are shown in the bottom panel of Table 2 (labelled "Unseen"). On EN-DEV, the best results are again obtained using BERT, however, the accuracy drops substantially on EN-TEST. RoBERTa performs more consistently across EN-DEV and EN-TEST, and performs best on EN-TEST. mBERT again performs relatively poorly compared to BERT and RoBERTa, but nevertheless substantially outperforms the most-frequent class baseline.

Focusing on the contribution of the CF feature, results for both BERT and RoBERTa on EN-DEV

---

[6]We do not consider the CF feature, which was developed for and evaluated on English VNCs (Fazly et al., 2009), for experiments with mBERT. We are primarily interested in mBERT as a point of comparison for cross-lingual experiments, and so do not incorporate this English-specific knowledge here. We also do not consider the CF feature in experiments on RUSSIAN or in cross-lingual experiments.

Setup	Model	EN-DEV		EN-TEST	
		−CF	+CF	−CF	+CF
All	MFC	63.4	63.4	62.9	62.9
	CForm	75.0	75.0	71.1	71.1
	King and Cook (2018)	82.5	85.6	81.5	84.7
	BERT	**90.7** ±0.53	**90.8** ±0.51	**89.3** ±1.11	**89.8** ±0.71
	RoBERTa	88.3 ±0.96	89.9 ±0.66	88.6 ±0.87	89.0 ±0.48
	mBERT	84.1 ±0.8	-	83.8 ±1.1	-
Unseen	MFC	60.9	60.9	63.3	63.3
	CForm	73.6	73.6	70.0	70.0
	King and Cook (2018)	72.3	76.4	74.6	77.8
	BERT	**83.5** ±0.97	**83.4** ±0.65	78.6 ±1.78	79.8 ±1.55
	RoBERTa	81.8 ±1.60	82.4 ±1.20	**82.3** ±1.76	**80.6** ±2.35
	mBERT	75.4 ±1.5	-	74.3 ±2.2	-

Table 2: % accuracy and standard deviation for the all and unseen expressions experimental setups on EN-DEV and EN-TEST, for BERT, RoBERTa, and mBERT, with and without the CF feature. % accuracy for the baselines is also shown. The best accuracy for each experimental setup, on each dataset, with and without the CF feature, is shown in boldface.

do not show a clear improvement when incorporating this feature when considering the standard deviation across runs. The impact of this feature in experiments on EN-TEST is similar. This finding again suggests that contextualized embeddings capture much of the linguistic knowledge encoded in this feature. We therefore focus on results for BERT and RoBERTa that do not incorporate the CF feature.

Focusing on results for EN-TEST (for which no hyper-parameter tuning was carried out), given the substantial improvements over the most-frequent class baseline, and over the CForm baseline, with the exception of mBERT when accounting for variation across runs, these findings suggest that the classifiers (including the approach of King and Cook) have learned information about the idiomaticity of PIEs, that is not restricted to specific expressions, as in the case of the all expressions experimental setup. Furthermore BERT and RoBERTa (without the CF feature) outperform the approach of King and Cook (2018), although given the standard deviation across runs, this difference does not appear to be significant for BERT when comparing against the approach of King and Cook when they use the CF feature.

In experiments until now we have used representations from the final layer of contextualized embedding models (BERT, RoBERTa, and mBERT). We now consider the effect of using different hidden layers, focusing on the unseen expressions ex-

Model	Dataset	Layer			
		9	10	11	12
BERT	EN-DEV	82.0	82.2	82.6	**83.5**
BERT	EN-TEST	79.2	79.8	**80.2**	78.6
RoBERTa	EN-DEV	75.6	78.2	79.8	**81.8**
RoBERTa	EN-TEST	71.8	77.7	79.5	**82.3**

Table 3: % accuracy and standard deviation for the unseen expressions experimental setup on EN-DEV and EN-TEST using BERT and RoBERTa with representations from the indicated layers. The best results for each model and dataset are shown in boldface.

perimental setup for BERT and RoBERTa, in an effort to explain the relatively poor performance of BERT here. Results are shown in Table 3.[7] In all cases, except for BERT on EN-TEST, the final layer performs best. This is inline with the findings of Jawahar et al. (2019) that the upper layers of BERT encode semantic information. For BERT, where accuracy was low on EN-TEST relative to EN-DEV in Table 2, on EN-TEST the second last layer performs best.

5.2 Russian

For monolingual experiments on Russian, we again consider the all and unseen expressions experimental setups. Here we compare against a most-frequent class baseline. Although Aharodnik et al.

---

[7]Results are only shown for layers 9–12. The overall trend for other layers is that lower layers achieve lower accuracy.

Setup	Model	% Accuracy
All	MFC	54.1
	RuBERT	87.4 ±4.7
	mBERT	**88.2** ±2.8
Unseen	MFC	54.3
	RuBERT	**74.6** ±2.2
	mBERT	73.6 ±3.8

Table 4: % accuracy and standard deviation for the all and unseen expressions experimental setups on RUSSIAN for RuBERT, mBERT, and the most-frequent class baseline (MFC). The best accuracy for each experimental setup is shown in boldface.

(2018) report preliminary results on this dataset, they are not for the same experimental setups that we consider, and so we do not compare against their results. Here we consider RuBERT, a monolingual Russian model, and mBERT, which includes Russian text in its pre-training. For the all and unseen expressions experimental setups we use the best hyper-parameter settings for EN-DEV using BERT for the unseen and all expressions experimental setups, respectively; i.e., we do not do any hyper-parameter tuning on RUSSIAN.

Results are shown in Table 4. We see that in both the all and unseen expressions experimental setups, both RuBERT and mBERT substantially outperform the most-frequent class baseline. We also see that, accounting for variation across runs, the performance of RuBERT and mBERT is similar within each experimental setup.

These findings add to those of Section 5.1, and again indicate that contextualized embeddings encode knowledge of PIE idiomaticity, although in this case the experiments consider a range of PIE syntactic constructions, as opposed to only VNCs. These findings also again indicate that the classifier for the unseen expressions experimental setup has learned information about the idiomaticity of PIEs that is not restricted to expressions that were observed during training. In the following section we consider whether contextualized embeddings encode knowledge of idiomaticity that can be generalized across languages.

6 Cross-lingual Results

In this section we consider cross-lingual experiments in which we train on instances of PIEs in a source language, and evaluate on instances of PIEs in a (different) target language. We consider the case of both English-to-Russian and Russian-to-English. For English we consider both EN-DEV and EN-TEST. In these experiments we train on the entire source language dataset (i.e., when Russian is the source language we train on RUSSIAN, and when English is the source language we train on either EN-DEV or EN-TEST), and evaluate on the entire target language dataset. We use the best hyper-parameter settings for EN-DEV using BERT for the unseen expressions experimental setup from Section 5.1; i.e., we do not attempt any hyper-parameter tuning for this cross-lingual experimental setup. We again compare results against a most-frequent class baseline, and when English is the target language, also against the unsupervised CForm baseline (Fazly et al., 2009).

Results are shown in Table 5. For English-to-Russian, and Russian-to-English, mBERT outperforms the most-frequent class baseline in each case. In experiments with English as the target language, mBERT also outperforms the CForm baseline, although in the case of EN-DEV the difference does not appear to be significant given the standard deviation across runs. Furthermore, the results are, remarkably, roughly on par with monolingual results for the unseen expressions experimental setup. Focusing on experiments involving EN-TEST and RUSSIAN, where for both datasets no hyper-parameter tuning was considered in previous experiments, for English-to-Russian (i.e., EN-TEST source, RUSSIAN target) mBERT achieves 72.4% accuracy, whereas in the monolingual Russian unseen expressions experimental setup, RuBERT and mBERT achieve accuracies of 74.6% and 73.6%, respectively (Table 4). These differences are relatively small considering the standard deviations across runs. For Russian-to-English (i.e., RUSSIAN source, EN-TEST target) mBERT achieves an accuracy of 80.1%, while the accuracies for contextualized embedding models for EN-TEST in the unseen expressions experimental setup range from 74.3% for mBERT to 82.3% for RoBERTa (Table 2).

Whereas the findings for the monolingual unseen expressions experimental setup indicate that the classifier is able to generalize to expressions that are unseen during training, these findings for cross-lingual experiments indicate that the classifier is able to generalize across languages. This suggests that the classifier has learned information about idiomaticity that is not restricted to specific expressions, nor to a specific language. The cross-

Source Language	Target language	Source dataset	Target dataset	Model	% Accuracy
English	Russian	EN-DEV	RUSSIAN	MFC	54.3
				mBERT	75.7 ±3.0
		EN-TEST	RUSSIAN	MFC	54.3
				mBERT	72.4 ±5.7
Russian	English	RUSSIAN	EN-DEV	MFC	60.9
				CForm	73.6
				mBERT	75.2 ±2.0
		RUSSIAN	EN-TEST	MFC	63.3
				CForm	70.0
				mBERT	80.1 ±1.3

Table 5: % accuracy and standard deviation for cross-lingual experiments from English to Russian (top panel) and Russian to English (bottom panel) using mBERT, a most-frequent class (MFC) baseline, and for English, the unsupervised CForm baseline.

lingual findings furthermore seem to be inline with the findings of Pires et al. (2019) that cross-lingual transfer with mBERT works reasonably well even when languages do not share the same script (as for English and Russian), but works less well when the languages do not share the same word order (where English is an SVO language, and Russian has freer word-order, but SVO is considered dominant (Dryer, 2013)).

7   Conclusions

In this paper we proposed a supervised model based on contextualized embeddings to predict the idiomaticity of PIE instances. In contrast to most prior work on this topic, we considered the ability of the model to generalize to expressions that were not observed during training, and also to generalize across languages. Code to reproduce these experiments is available.[8]

We first considered monolingual experiments for English, focusing on verb–noun combinations, a common type of PIE. In experiments in which we train and test on instances of the same PIEs, we demonstrated that an approach based on contextualized embeddings improves over previous approaches based on conventional word embeddings. We then considered experiments in which we evaluate on PIEs that were not observed during training, and showed that the proposed approach improves over a strong, linguistically-informed unsupervised baseline. We further found that, in con-

trast to prior models based on conventional word embeddings, incorporating information about the lexico-syntactic fixedness of VNCs does not lead to clear improvements, suggesting that contextualized embeddings capture this rich linguistic knowledge.

In monolingual experiments on Russian we considered a wider range of types of PIEs. Here we showed that, as for English, the proposed approach improves over baselines when evaluating on expressions that were, and were not, observed during training. The experimental setup in which the model is tested on instances of PIE types that were not observed during training is particularly interesting because we do not expect to have annotated instances of all PIE types available for training supervised models. The findings in this experimental setup, for both English and Russian, indicate that the model is capturing knowledge of PIE idiomaticity that is not restricted to specific expressions.

Finally, we considered cross-lingual experiments in which we train on instances of either English or Russian PIEs, and evaluate on PIE instances in the other language. Here the proposed model again improves over baselines, and achieves performance that is roughly on par with that of monolingual experiments in which we evaluate on PIEs that were not observed during training. This finding indicates that contextualized embeddings encode knowledge of PIE idiomaticity that is not restricted to specific expressions, nor to a specific language.

In future work, we plan to further explore cross-lingual idiomaticity prediction. We would like to include more languages in the analysis to be able to measure the impact of training on multiple source languages. We further intend to consider including

---

[8]`https://github.com/SaminFakharian/Contextualized-Embeddings-Encode-Monolingual-and-Cross-lingual-Knowledge-of-Idiomaticity`

the target language amongst the source languages, to measure the impact of augmenting training data for the target language with data from other languages. Finally, we intend to consider cross-lingual approaches for other MWE prediction tasks, such as predicting noun compound compositionality.

Acknowledgments

This work is financially supported by the Natural Sciences and Engineering Research Council of Canada, the New Brunswick Innovation Foundation (NBIF), and the University of New Brunswick.

References

Katsiaryna Aharodnik, Anna Feldman, and Jing Peng. 2018. Designing a Russian idiom-annotated corpus. In *Proceedings of the Eleventh International Conference on Language Resources and Evaluation (LREC 2018)*, Miyazaki, Japan. European Language Resources Association (ELRA).

Timothy Baldwin and Su Nam Kim. 2010. Multiword expressions. In Nitin Indurkhya and Fred J. Damerau, editors, *Handbook of Natural Language Processing*, 2nd edition. CRC Press, Boca Raton, USA.

Lou Burnard. 2000. *The British National Corpus Users Reference Guide*. Oxford University Computing Services.

Paul Cook, Afsaneh Fazly, and Suzanne Stevenson. 2008. The VNC-Tokens Dataset. In *Proceedings of the LREC Workshop on Towards a Shared Task for Multiword Expressions (MWE 2008)*, pages 19–22, Marrakech, Morocco.

Jacob Devlin, Ming-Wei Chang, Kenton Lee, and Kristina Toutanova. 2019. BERT: Pre-training of deep bidirectional transformers for language understanding. In *Proceedings of the 2019 Conference of the North American Chapter of the Association for Computational Linguistics: Human Language Technologies, Volume 1 (Long and Short Papers)*, pages 4171–4186, Minneapolis, Minnesota. Association for Computational Linguistics.

Matthew S. Dryer. 2013. Order of subject, object and verb. In Matthew S. Dryer and Martin Haspelmath, editors, *The World Atlas of Language Structures Online*. Max Planck Institute for Evolutionary Anthropology, Leipzig.

Afsaneh Fazly, Paul Cook, and Suzanne Stevenson. 2009. Unsupervised type and token identification of idiomatic expressions. *Computational Linguistics*, 35(1):61–103.

Waseem Gharbieh, Virendra Bhavsar, and Paul Cook. 2016. A word embedding approach to identifying verb-noun idiomatic combinations. In *Proceedings*

of the 12th Workshop on Multiword Expressions, pages 112–118, Berlin, Germany. Association for Computational Linguistics.

Hessel Haagsma, Malvina Nissim, and Johan Bos. 2018. The other side of the coin: Unsupervised disambiguation of potentially idiomatic expressions by contrasting senses. In *Proceedings of the Joint Workshop on Linguistic Annotation, Multiword Expressions and Constructions (LAW-MWE-CxG-2018)*, pages 178–184, Santa Fe, New Mexico, USA. Association for Computational Linguistics.

Reyhaneh Hashempour and Aline Villavicencio. 2020. Leveraging contextual embeddings and idiom principle for detecting idiomaticity in potentially idiomatic expressions. In *Proceedings of the Workshop on the Cognitive Aspects of the Lexicon*, pages 72–80, Online. Association for Computational Linguistics.

Pierre Isabelle, Colin Cherry, and George Foster. 2017. A challenge set approach to evaluating machine translation. In *Proceedings of the 2017 Conference on Empirical Methods in Natural Language Processing*, pages 2486–2496, Copenhagen, Denmark. Association for Computational Linguistics.

Ganesh Jawahar, Benoît Sagot, and Djamé Seddah. 2019. What does BERT learn about the structure of language? In *Proceedings of the 57th Annual Meeting of the Association for Computational Linguistics*, pages 3651–3657, Florence, Italy. Association for Computational Linguistics.

Milton King and Paul Cook. 2018. Leveraging distributed representations and lexico-syntactic fixedness for token-level prediction of the idiomaticity of English verb-noun combinations. In *Proceedings of the 56th Annual Meeting of the Association for Computational Linguistics (Volume 2: Short Papers)*, pages 345–350, Melbourne, Australia. Association for Computational Linguistics.

Diederik P. Kingma and Jimmy Ba. 2015. Adam: A method for stochastic optimization. In *3rd International Conference on Learning Representations, ICLR 2015, San Diego, CA, USA, May 7-9, 2015, Conference Track Proceedings*.

Ryan Kiros, Yukun Zhu, Ruslan Salakhutdinov, Richard S. Zemel, Antonio Torralba, Raquel Urtasun, and Sanja Fidler. 2015. Skip-thought vectors. In C. Cortes, N. D. Lawrence, D. D. Lee, M. Sugiyama, and R. Garnett, editors, *Advances in Neural Information Processing Systems 28*, pages 3276–3284. Curran Associates, Inc.

Yuri Kuratov and Mikhail Arkhipov. 2019. Adaptation of deep bidirectional multilingual transformers for russian language. *arXiv preprint arXiv:1905.07213*.

Murathan Kurfalı and Robert Östling. 2020. Disambiguation of potentially idiomatic expressions with contextual embeddings. In *Proceedings of the Joint*

Workshop on Multiword Expressions and Electronic Lexicons, pages 85–94, online. Association for Computational Linguistics.

Changsheng Liu and Rebecca Hwa. 2018. Heuristically informed unsupervised idiom usage recognition. In *Proceedings of the 2018 Conference on Empirical Methods in Natural Language Processing*, pages 1723–1731, Brussels, Belgium. Association for Computational Linguistics.

Yinhan Liu, Myle Ott, Naman Goyal, Jingfei Du, Mandar Joshi, Danqi Chen, Omer Levy, Mike Lewis, Luke Zettlemoyer, and Veselin Stoyanov. 2019. Roberta: A robustly optimized bert pretraining approach. *arXiv preprint arXiv:1907.11692*.

Oren Melamud, Jacob Goldberger, and Ido Dagan. 2016. context2vec: Learning generic context embedding with bidirectional LSTM. In *Proceedings of The 20th SIGNLL Conference on Computational Natural Language Learning*, pages 51–61, Berlin, Germany. Association for Computational Linguistics.

Telmo Pires, Eva Schlinger, and Dan Garrette. 2019. How multilingual is multilingual BERT? In *Proceedings of the 57th Annual Meeting of the Association for Computational Linguistics*, pages 4996–5001, Florence, Italy. Association for Computational Linguistics.

Giancarlo Salton, Robert Ross, and John Kelleher. 2016. Idiom token classification using sentential distributed semantics. In *Proceedings of the 54th Annual Meeting of the Association for Computational Linguistics (Volume 1: Long Papers)*, pages 194–204, Berlin, Germany. Association for Computational Linguistics.

Vered Shwartz and Ido Dagan. 2019. Still a pain in the neck: Evaluating text representations on lexical composition. *Transactions of the Association for Computational Linguistics*, 7:403–419.

Thomas Wolf, Lysandre Debut, Victor Sanh, Julien Chaumond, Clement Delangue, Anthony Moi, Pierric Cistac, Tim Rault, Remi Louf, Morgan Funtowicz, Joe Davison, Sam Shleifer, Patrick von Platen, Clara Ma, Yacine Jernite, Julien Plu, Canwen Xu, Teven Le Scao, Sylvain Gugger, Mariama Drame, Quentin Lhoest, and Alexander Rush. 2020. Transformers: State-of-the-art natural language processing. In *Proceedings of the 2020 Conference on Empirical Methods in Natural Language Processing: System Demonstrations*, pages 38–45, Online. Association for Computational Linguistics.

PIE: A Parallel Idiomatic Expression Corpus for Idiomatic Sentence Generation and Paraphrasing

Jianing Zhou[1], Hongyu Gong[2] and Suma Bhat[1]
[1]University of Illinois at Urbana-Champaign
[2]Facebook AI
`{zjn1746, spbhat2}@illinois.edu`
`hygong@fb.com`

Abstract

Idiomatic expressions (IE) play an important role in natural language, and have long been a "pain in the neck" for NLP systems. Despite this, text generation tasks related to IEs remain largely under-explored. In this paper, we propose two new tasks of idiomatic sentence generation and paraphrasing to fill this research gap. We introduce a curated dataset of 823 IEs, and a parallel corpus with sentences containing them and the same sentences where the IEs were replaced by their literal paraphrases as the primary resource for our tasks. We benchmark existing deep learning models, which have state-of-the-art performance on related tasks using automated and manual evaluation with our dataset to inspire further research on our proposed tasks. By establishing baseline models, we pave the way for more comprehensive and accurate modeling of IEs, both for generation and paraphrasing.[1]

1 Introduction

Idiomatic expressions (IEs) make language natural. These are multiword expressions (MWEs) that are non-compositional because their meaning differs from the literal meaning of their constituent words taken together (Nunberg et al., 1994). Their use imparts naturalness and fluency (Wray and Perkins, 2000; Sprenger, 2003; Pawley and Syder, 2014; Schmitt and Schmitt, 2020), is prompted by pragmatic and topical functions in discourse (Simpson and Mendis, 2003) and often conveys a nuance in expression (stylistic enhancement) using imagery that is beyond what is available in the context (Nunberg et al., 1994). Idiomatic expressions, including phrasal verbs (e.g., carry out), idioms (e.g., pull one's leg) are also an essential part of a native speakers vocabulary and lexicon (Jackendoff, 1995).

English	Vote them out!
Spanish	¡Vote para sacarlos!
Arabic	!التصويت لهم
Chinese	投票给他们！
Hindi	उन्हें वोट दें!
French	Votez-les!
German	Stimmen Sie sie ab!
Korean	투표하세요!
Russian	Проголосуйте за них!

Figure 1: State-of-the-art machine translations of "Vote them out!" into different languages mean the opposite.

IEs constitute a ubiquitous part of daily language and social communication, primarily used in conversation, fiction and news (Biber et al., 1999), frequently used by teachers when presenting their lessons to students (Kerbel and Grunwell, 1997) and occur cross-lingually (Baldwin et al., 2010; Nunberg et al., 1994). Their non-compositionality is the reason for their classical standing as "a pain in the neck" (Sag et al., 2002) and "hard going" (Rayson et al., 2010) for NLP.

The Oxford English dictionary defines the phrasal verb (an IE) *vote out* as 'To turn (a person) out of office.' Using Google translate[2] to translate the topical slogan "vote them out!" into eight of the world's most spoken and relatively resource-rich languages yielded the results shown in Figure 1. As native speakers will attest, other than in Spanish, all the translations mean just the opposite, "vote for them!" This, and other studies on computational processing of idioms and metaphors in (Salton et al., 2014; Shao et al.; Shutova et al., 2013) reinforce the need for nuanced language processing—a grand challenge for NLP systems.

Gaining a deeper understanding of IEs and their

---

[1]The parallel corpus is available at `https://github.com/zhjjn/MWE_PIE.git`

[2]`https://translate.google.com/`. Accessed November 19, 2020

33

Proceedings of the 17th Workshop on Multiword Expressions, pages 33–48
Bangkok, Thailand (online), August 6, 2021. ©2021 Association for Computational Linguistics

literal counterparts is an important step toward this goal. In this paper, we introduce two novel tasks related to paraphrasing between literal and idiomatic expressions in unrestricted text: (1) Idiomatic sentence simplification (ISS) to automatically paraphrase idiomatic expressions in text, and 2) Idiomatic sentence generation (ISG) to replace a literal phrase in a sentence with a synonymous but more vivid phrase (e.g., an idiom). ISS directly addresses the need for performing text simplification in several application settings, including summarizers (Klebanov et al., 2004) and parsing (Constant et al., 2017). Moreover, ISS may actually be helpful when an idiomatic expression does not have an exact counterpart in a target language. This is akin to the 'translation by paraphrase' strategy recommended for human translation when the source language idiom is obscure and non-existent in the target language (Baker, 2018). On the other hand, ISG advances the area of text style transfer (Jhamtani et al., 2017; Gong et al., 2019) bringing the as yet unexplored dimension of nuanced language to style transfer.

A second important component of this paper is the introduction of a new curated dataset of parallel idiomatic and literal sentences, where the idiomatic expressions are paraphrased, created for the purpose of advancing progress in nuanced language processing and serving as a testbed for the proposed tasks. Recent literature has explored several aspects of figurative and nonliteral language processing, including detecting and interpreting metaphors (Shutova, 2010b; Shutova et al., 2013), disambiguating IEs for their figurative or literal in a given context (Constant et al., 2017; Savary et al., 2017; Liu and Hwa, 2019) and analyzing sarcasm (Muresan et al., 2016; Joshi et al., 2017; Ghosh et al., 2018), by using curated datasets of sentences with linguistic processes in the wild. These datasets are ill-suited for the proposed tasks because they consist of specific figurative constructions (metaphors) (Shutova, 2010a), do not cover multiple IEs (Cook et al., 2008; Korkontzelos et al., 2013), or are not parallel (Haagsma et al., 2020; Savary et al., 2017) underscoring the need for a new dataset.

The newly constructed dataset permits us to benchmark the performance of several state-of-the-art neural network architectures (seq2seq and pretrained+fine-tuned models, with and without copy-enrichment) that have demonstrated compet-itive performance in the related tasks of simplification, and style transfer. Using automatic and manual evaluations of the outputs for the two tasks, we find that the existing models are inadequate for the proposed tasks. The sequence-to-sequence models clearly suffer from data sparsity, the added copy mechanism helps preserve the context that is not replaced, and despite their prior knowledge of the pretrained models, they are still limited in their ability to paraphrase and generate. This leads us to discussing novel insights, applications and future directions for related research.

The main contributions of this work are summarized as follows.

1. We propose two new tasks related to idiomatic expressions—idiomatic sentence simplification and idiomatic sentence generation;

2. We introduce a curated dataset of 823 idiomatic expressions, replete with sentences containing these IEs in the wild and the same sentences where the IEs were replaced by their literal paraphrases.

3. We use the combination of the new dataset and the proposed tasks as a lens through which we gain novel insights about the capabilities of deep learning models for processing nuanced language generation and paraphrasing.

2   Task Definition

We propose two new tasks: **idiomatic sentence generation** transforms a literal sentence into a sentence involving idioms. Used frequently in everyday language, idioms are known to add color to expressions and improve the fluency of communication. The idiomatic rewriting improves the quality of text generation in that it could enhance the textual diversity and convey abstract and complicated ideas in a succinct manner. For example, the idiomatic sentence *BP cut corners and violated safety requirements* conveys the same idea as its literal counterpart *BP saved time, money and energy and violated safety requirements*, but in a more vivid and succinct manner.

The second task is **idiomatic sentence paraphrasing**, simplifying sentences with idioms into literal expressions. As an example, the sentence– *It is certainly not a sensible move to cut corners with national security*– has the idiom *cut corners* replaced the literal counterpart *save money*. By paraphrasing the idioms from which machine translation often suffers, our task of idiomatic sentence paraphrasing can also benefit machine translation.

In this work, we distinguish our task of idiomatic sentence generation from idiom generation. While the latter task creates new idioms with novel word combinations, our study is to use existing idioms in a sentence and preserve the semantic meaning.

The task of idiomatic sentence paraphrasing is closely related to text simplification that has mostly been studied as related tasks of lexical paraphrasing and syntactic paraphrasing (Xu et al., 2015). A significant departure of this task from that of these related tasks that centrally address style is that (i) we aim for local synonymous paraphrasing by transforming not the entire sentence but a phrase in the sentence, (ii) the transformation is not related to syntactic structures, but related to the complexity in meaning[3]. We propose doing joint monolingual translation with simplification and is similar in spirit to (Agrawal and Carpuat, 2020).

There are many technical challenges to performing these tasks. The task of idiomatic sentence paraphrasing involves first identifying that an expression is an idiom and not a literal expression (e.g. *black sheep*) (Fazly et al., 2009; Korkontzelos et al., 2013; Liu and Hwa, 2019). Once identified, the IE may have multiple senses (e.g. *tick off*) and its appropriate sense will need to be identified before paraphrasing it. Third, an appropriate literal phrase will have to be generated to replace the IE. Finally, the literal phrase will have to be fit in the surrounding sentential context for a fluent construction. For idiomatic sentence generation, the context of the literal phrase could permit more than one candidate idiom (e.g. keep quiet). In this study, we assume that we have an idiomatic sentence and leave it to future work to explore the task in conjunction with this step.

3 Related Work

The theme of this paper is naturally connected to three streams of text generation tasks—paraphrasing, style transfer and metaphoric expression generation. We will discuss these tasks and also the datasets used in these tasks to study their similarities and differences to our dataset and tasks.

3.1 Paraphrase

The aim of paraphrasing is to rewrite a given sentence while preserving its original meaning. Being widely studied in the recent research, many datasets have been constructed to facilitate the task. PPDB (Ganitkevitch et al., 2013), MRPC [4], Twitter URL Corpus (Lan et al., 2017), Quora [5] and ParaNMT-50M (Wieting and Gimpel, 2017) have been the most commonly used datasets. The most commonly used Seq2Seq models have been successfully applied to paraphrasing Prakash et al. (2016); Gupta et al. (2018); Iyyer et al. (2018); Yang et al. (2019). Besides the end-to-end models, a template-based pipeline model was proposed to divide paraphrase generation into template extraction, template transforming and template filling (Gu et al., 2019).

However, unlike paraphrasing a sentence or a literal-to-literal paraphrasing task, our proposed tasks are more constrained given the existence of idiomatic expressions. This renders the datasets used for the task of paraphrasing and the associated paraphrasing models inadequate for our task. Our dataset is created to fill this need to advance a fundamental understanding of idiomatic text generation and paraphrasing. Therefore, research into our tasks and dataset can also be used for paraphrasing when only part of the sentence need to be paraphrased or idioms need to be paraphrased.

3.2 Style Transfer

The task of style transfer can be defined as rewriting sentences into those with a target style. Recent research has primarily focused sentiment manipulation and changes in writing styles (Jhamtani et al., 2017; Gong et al., 2019). Our proposed tasks are different from the nature of style transfer studies in recent works because (i) our tasks retain a large portion of the input sentences while style transfer may need to completely change the input sentences, and (ii) our tasks explore the nuance component of style, an aspect heretofore unexplored. To test different models' performance on style transfer, several non-parallel corpora have been used (Yelp (Shen et al., 2017), Grammarly's Yahoo Answers Formality Corpus (Rao and Tetreault, 2018), Amazon Food Review dataset (McAuley and Leskovec, 2013) and Product Review dataset (He and McAuley, 2016)).

---

[3]The consideration of whether idioms are semantic- or pragmatic- or discourse-level phenomena is important, but beyond the scope of this paper.

[4]https://www.microsoft.com/en-us/download/details.aspx?id=52398

[5]https://www.kaggle.com/aymenmouelhi/quora-duplicate-questions

Despite their size, they lack the focus on IEs and are all non-parallel. This has led to the the study of unsupervised methods for style transfer, including cross-aligned auto-encoder (Hu et al., 2017), VAE (Hu et al., 2017), Generative Adversarial Network (Zeng et al., 2020), reinforcement learning for constraints in style transfer (Xu et al., 2018; Gong et al., 2019) and pipeline models (Li et al., 2018; Sudhakar et al., 2019). Owing to the essential departure of our tasks from those of previously studied style transfer tasks, and the limitation of non-parallel corpus, we create our own parallel dataset which focuses on IEs.

3.3 Metaphoric Expression Generation

Prior work on automated metaphor processing has primarily focused on their identification, interpretation and also generation. (Shutova, 2010b; Shutova et al., 2013; Abe et al., 2006). Also, data for this task is extremely sparse: there are not any large scale parallel corpora containing literal and metaphoric paraphrases which aims for metaphor generation. The most useful one is that of (Mohammad et al., 2016). However, their dataset has a small number (171) of metaphoric sentences extracted from WordNet. Early works on metaphor generation mainly focus on phrase level metaphor and template-based generation (Terai and Nakagawa, 2010; Ovchinnikova et al., 2014). Recent works also explore the power of neural networks (Mao et al., 2018; Yu and Wan, 2019; Stowe et al., 2020). However, most of the research on metaphor generation suffer from the lack of parallel corpora.

Our proposed tasks share some similarities with metaphor generation but also have differences. Instead of focusing on paraphrase of single word like most metaphor generation work, our tasks often require a mapping between two multi-word expressions, which makes our tasks more challenging.

3.4 Text Simplification

Text simplification aims to rewrite input sentences into lexically and/or syntactically simplified forms. The Simple Wikipedia Corpus (Zhu et al., 2010) and more recently, the Newsela dataset (Xu et al., 2015) and the WikiLarge dataset (Zhang and Lapata, 2017) dominate the research area. The use of different machine learning models have also been explored for this task, including statistical machine translation model (Wubben et al., 2012), the Seq2Seq architecture (Nisioi et al., 2017) and the Transformer architecture (Zhao et al., 2018).

Departing from previous attempts at lexical or syntactic simplification, our proposed task of idiomatic sentence paraphrasing aims to simplify the nuance of non-compositional and figurative expressions thereby permitting a more literal understanding of the sentence.

We summarize the datasets of the related tasks in Table 1.

4 Building the Dataset

We describe the details of the data collection, data annotation, corpus analyses and comparisons with other existing corpora.

4.1 Data Collection

The Parallel Idiomatic Expression Corpus (PIE), consists of idiomatic expressions (IEs), their definitions, sentences containing the IEs and corresponding sentences where the IEs are replaced with their literal paraphrases. One instance of the dataset is shown in Figure 2.

We collected a list of 1042 popular IEs and their meanings from an educational website [6] that has a broad coverage of frequently used IEs including phrasal verbs, idioms and proverbs. For a broad coverage of IEs we did not limit them to a specific syntactic category. The list was then split between the members of the research team consisting of a native English speaker, and three near-native English speakers. Some IEs such as "tick off" (Figure 2) have multiple senses. The annotators labeled the sense of IEs in given sentences according to the sense information from reliable sources including the Oxford English Dictionary[7], the Webster Dictionary [8] and the Longman Dictionary of Contemporary English[9]. IEs that were not available in any of the popular dictionaries were excluded from dataset as were proverbs that are independent clauses (e.g., *the pen is mightier than the sword*). To guarantee each sense is well represented, the annotators collected at least 5 sentences for each sense of an IE from online sources (e.g., the Contemporary corpus of American English, and examples listed in dictionaries).

The data collection step yielded the corpus with a total of 823 IEs and 5170 sentence-pairs using these IEs (an average of 6.3 sentence-pairs per id-

---

[6]www.theidioms.com
[7]https://www.oxfordlearnersdictionaries.com
[8]https://www.merriam-webster.com
[9]https://www.ldoceonline.com

Idiom	Tick Off	
Sense	to complete an item on a list	to make someone angry or offended
Idiomatic Sentence	I would like to tick off some more items on my list before going home	My decision is going to tick off my entire family.
Idiomatic Labels	O O O O **B I** O O O O O O O O	O O O O O **B I** O O O.
Literal Sentence	I would like to cross out some more items on my list before going home	My decision is going to anger my entire family.
Literal Labels	O O O O **B I** O O O O O O O O	O O O O O **B** O O O.

Figure 2: An example from our dataset. Idioms are highlighted in blue, and their literal paraphrases are in red.

iom). We also note that every instance (idiomatic-literal pair) is only one sentence long. The corpus statistics are summarized in Table 2.

4.2 Data Annotation

In order to create the parallel dataset of idiomatic and literal sentences for the proposed tasks, a native English speaker was asked to rewrite each idiomatic sentence into its literal form, where the IE was replaced by a literal phrase. As part of this manual paraphrasing, the annotator was asked to paraphrase only the IE so as not to alter its meaning in the context of the sentence, preserving the phrases syntactic function and to conform to the sense definition. The rest of the sentence was to be left unchanged. The annotator is free to use original sense definition when rewriting or use paraphrases of sense definition. After the first annotation pass, the researchers checked the literal sentences generated by the first annotator and corrected any errors.

To specify the span of the IE in each idiomatic sentence and that of the literal paraphrase in the corresponding literal sentence, **BIO** labels were used; **B** marks the beginning of the idiom expressions (resp. the literal paraphrases), **I** the other words in the IE (resp. words in the literal paraphrases) and **O** all the other words in the sentences. This labeling was done automatically considering that the only difference between a given idiomatic sentence and its literal sentence is the replacement of idiom with literal phrase. An example of the **BIO** labeled sentence pair is shown in Figure 2.

4.3 Corpus Analyses

We summarize the statistics of our PIE dataset in Table 2 and compare it with existing datasets in Table 1. We notice that the parallel sentences in our dataset are comparable in terms of sentence length, while simple sentences are much shorter in the text simplification dataset. This suggests that the tasks we propose may not result in significantly shorter sentences compared to their inputs, and this constitutes a core departure from the task of text simplification. Moreover, the sentences in our dataset are longer on an average compared to the sentences in existing datasets (with the exception of text simplification data). This can pose challenges to the text generation model performing the tasks proposed in the paper.

We also report the percentage of n-grams in the literal sentences which do not appear in the idiomatic sentences as a measure of the difference between the idiomatic and literal sentences. As shown in Table 3, there is smaller variation between the source sentences and the target sentences in our dataset. This is again due to the nature of our task, which calls for a local paraphrasing (rewriting only a part of the sentence).

We note that IEs may be naturally ambiguous due to the existence of both figurative and literal senses, as also pointed out in previous works. A small portion of IEs in our dataset have multiple senses, and one example is "tick off " in Figure 2. Table 4 presents the distribution of the senses in the IEs in our dataset, and the average number of senses is 1.05, suggesting that the majority IEs in our dataset are monosemous.

4.4 Dataset quality

Noting that the idiomatic to literal sentences were manually created, the quality of our dataset may be called into question. We point out that in an effort to quickly use sentences of good quality and in line with existing datasets for related tasks with idiomatic expressions (Haagsma et al., 2020; Korkontzelos et al., 2013) we collected idiomatic expressions in the wild. However, as acknowledged by previous dataset creation efforts, not all IEs oc-

Dataset	Parallel	Task	Size	# idioms	Sent Len (original)	Sent Len (target)
PIE (ours)	✔	Idiom Generation/Paraphrasing	3,524/823/823	823	18.5	19.0
Para-NMT	✔	Paraphrase	5,370,128	-	11.43	10.56
WikiLarge	✔	Text Simplification	296,402/992/359	-	24.1	15.51
Metaphor	✔	Metaphor Generation	171	-	7.30	7.37

Table 1: Comparison of our dataset with related datasets. Training, validation and testing size splits are provided when applicable. Data in all these datasets is a combination of collection from the wild and manual generation. In our corpus, original sentences are idiomatic sentences and target sentences are literal sentences.

Statistics	# of instances	Avg. # of words
Idioms	823	3.2
Sense	862	7.9
Idiomatic sent	5170	19.0
Literal sent	5170	18.5

Table 2: Statistics of our parallel corpus.

% n-grams	PIE	Para-NMT	Wiki-Large	Metaphor
uni-grams	13.86	46.34	36.2	16.88
bi-grams	23.60	71.24	52.56	36.59
tri-grams	30.19	82.26	58.75	59.61
4-grams	36.51	86.46	62.79	74.41

Table 3: The percentage of n-grams in source sentences which do not appear in the target sentences. In our case, it is the percentage of n-grams in literal sentences which do not appear in the idiomatic sentences.

# senses	# of idioms	# pairs	Avg. # of words
1	788	4788	3.2
2	31	322	2.6
3	4	60	2.0

Table 4: Statistics of sense distribution. An idiom has an average of 1.05 senses.

cur equally frequently, which can result in a representation bias. In addition, finding true paraphrases of IEs in the wild is hard. In light of these practical data-related concerns, we resorted to a manual paraphrasing of the IEs as a trade-off between naturalness and representation. This idea of using non-natural instances is also influenced by successful recent approaches to training data collection and data augmentation using synthetic methods reported in severely resource-constrained domains such as machine translation (Sennrich et al., 2016) and clinical language processing (Ive et al., 2020).

5 Experiments

5.1 Baselines

Translation Models: Considering that our tasks of idiomatic sentence generation and paraphrasing have never been studied before and the fact that they are both text generation tasks, we first choose some basic end-to-end models which have shown state-of-the-art performance on other text generation tasks. Accordingly, we used the LSTM-based Seq2Seq model (Sutskever et al., 2014) and the transformer architecture (Vaswani et al., 2017). These will be alluded to as **Translation Models.**

Copy Models: Because the idiomatic sentences and their literal counterparts have identical context words, we consider the context to remain unchanged during generation. This prompts the use of the copy-enriched seq2seq model (Jhamtani et al., 2017) and the transformer model with a copy mechanism (Gehrmann et al., 2018) [10] (hereafter collectively called **Copy Models**).

BART: Considering the similarity between our tasks and paraphrasing, we also choose the pre-trained BART (Lewis et al., 2019), successfully used for text simplification and paraphrasing. We fine-tuned it on our training instances.

Pipeline Model: Finally, we used a sequential model inspired by the retrieve-delete-generate pipeline (Sudhakar et al., 2019; Zhou et al., 2021) that showed a competitive performance for style transfer. We note that novel instances of idiomatic sentences cannot be generated without previously encountering the IE. Considering this, we set up the pipeline model with a retrieval stage to retrieve an IE for a given literal sentence (resp. the correct sense given an idiomatic sentence). Toward this, a RoBERTa model for sentence classification was fine-tuned on our training data. The concatenation of the input sentence and the correct idiom or sense is considered as a positive instance and that of the input sentence and an irrelevant idiom or a different sense is considered a negative instance. Given all the concatenations of the input sentence and the idioms in our dataset, this stage aims to classify the correct one. In the deletion stage, we deleted the literal phrase that should have been replaced by the retrieved idioms (resp. deleted the IE in the given

[10]https://github.com/lipiji/TranSummar

idiomatic sentence). Again, a RoBERTa model for sequence classification was fine-tuned on our training data with **BIO** labels. This stage aims to assign one of the **BIO** labels for each token in the input sentence and delete the tokens with labels of **B** and **I**. In the generating stage, we combined the results from the retrieval and deletion stages and use a fine-tuned BART model to generate final output— the literal sentences for the task of idiomatic sentence paraphrasing and idiomatic sentences for the task of idiomatic sentence generation.

5.2 Experimental Setup

For all the models, the maximum sentence length was set to 128. The batch size and base learning rates were set to 32 and $5e - 5$ respectively. These models were all trained and run on the Google Colab platform.

For the translation models and copy models, the dimension of the hidden state vectors was set to 256 and the dimension of the word embeddings to 256. These baselines were trained with the parallel sentence pairs as appropriate, i.e., taking literal sentences as input and generating the corresponding idiomatic sentences or vice versa.

The baseline pretrained BART model was trained for 5 epochs and during inference a beam search with 5 beams was used with top-k set to 100 and top-p set to 0.5. The other hyper-parameters were set to their default values.

All the RoBerta and BART models in the pipeline model were trained for 5 epochs. For the BART model, during inference, we used a beam search with 5 beams with top-k set to 100 and top-p set to 0.5. The other hyper-parameters were set to their default values.

5.3 Evaluation

For automatic evaluation, Rouge (Lin, 2004), BLEU (Papineni et al., 2002), METEOR (Lavie and Agarwal, 2007) and SARI (Xu et al., 2016) are used to compare the similarity between the generated sentences and the references. These metrics has been widely used in various text generation tasks such as paraphrasing, style transfer and text simplification. To measure linguistic quality, we use a pre-trained language model BERT to calculate perplexity scores and a recently proposed measure, GRUEN (Zhu and Bhat, 2020).

Considering that automatic evaluation cannot fully analyze the results, we use human evaluation as a complement to the automatic evaluation metrics. For each task, We randomly sampled 100 input sentences and the corresponding outputs of all baselines. Human annotations were collected with respect to context, style and fluency of generated sentences based on the following criteria.

(1) **Context preservation** measures how well the context surrounding the idiomatic/literal phrase is preserved in the output.

(2) **Target inclusion** checks whether the correct IE or literal phrase is used in the output.

(3) **Fluency** evaluates the fluency and readability of the output sentence including how appropriately the verb tense, noun and pronoun forms are used.

(4) **Overall meaning** evaluates the overall quality of the output sentence.

For each output sentence, two annotators with native-speaker-level English proficiency were asked to rate it on a scale from 1 to 6 in terms of the context preservation, fluency and overall meaning. Higher scores indicate better quality. As for the target inclusion, they were asked to rate it on a scale from 1 to 3. Score 1 denotes that the target phrase is not included in the input at all, 2 denotes partial inclusion, and 3 is for the complete inclusion. We report the average score over all samples for each baseline in each aspect.

6 Results and Discussion

Results. We report the automatic and human evaluation results in Table 5 and 6. More detailed results with all the metrics considered are in the appendix. On both tasks, going by the automatic metrics, copy-enriched transformer, pretrained BART model and the pipeline model perform better than other baselines. Pretrained BART achieved the best performance in BLEU and GRUEN, and the pipeline model does best in SARI. As for human evaluation, BART and the pipeline again achieve the best performance among the baselines. While BART is the best in preserving contexts and achieving fluency, the pipeline is the best in idiom paraphrasing and generation. The overall agreement score for human evaluation is 0.76.

Model competence. BART and the pipeline model outperform other baselines in that they leverage auxiliary information (large pretaining corpora and selective idiomatic expression information, respectively) which is not available to the other models. The benefit of the copy mechanism by explicitly retaining the contexts as required by our tasks, is

Model	BLEU		SARI		GRUEN	
	s2i	i2s	s2i	i2s	s2i	i2s
Seq2Seq	25.16	42.96	24.13	33.89	32.25	33.45
Seq2Seq with copy	38.02	47.58	43.02	49.69	27.79	32.84
Transformer	45.58	46.65	36.67	38.62	44.05	44.06
Transformer with copy	59.56	57.91	39.93	45.10	59.27	52.25
Pretrained BART	**79.32**	**78.53**	62.30	61.82	**77.49**	**78.03**
Pipeline	65.56	70.03	**67.64**	**62.45**	67.27	74.16

Table 5: Automatic evaluation results for the task of idiomatic sentence generation (**s2i**) and idiomatic sentence paraphrasing (**i2s**).

Model	Context		Target		Fluency		Overall	
	s2i	i2s	s2i	i2s	s2i	i2s	s2i	i2s
Seq2Seq	1.3	1.2	1.1	1.1	1.1	1.0	1.7	1.7
Seq2Seq with copy	3.8	3.8	1.6	1.7	2.1	3.4	3.5	3.6
Transformer	4.2	4.3	1.3	1.2	3.3	3.4	3.4	3.3
Transformer with copy	5.4	5.3	1.2	1.6	4.6	4.6	3.9	4.2
Pretrained BART	**5.9**	**5.9**	1.5	2.1	**5.9**	**5.9**	4.4	5.0
Pipeline	5.6	5.8	**1.7**	**2.2**	5.1	5.3	**4.5**	**5.1**

Table 6: Human evaluation results for the two tasks.

shown in the corresponding gains in automatic and manual evaluation scores for both Seq2Seq and transformer models.

When it comes to the comparison between BART and the pipeline, BART does better in retaining the contexts surrounding idiomatic expressions given its high context score in human evaluation while the pipeline is better at handling the idiomatic part, i.e., target inclusion. Despite the reported superior performance of BART in related text generation tasks (Lewis et al., 2019), our experiments show that BART has limited capability in idiom paraphrasing and generation. The pipeline method, by virtue of error propagation from its retrieval and deletion modules suffers in terms of both the context preservation and fluency. For task of idiomatic sentence generation, the accuracy for retrieval module is 0.27 and F1 score for deletion module is 0.68. For task of idiomatic sentence paraphrasing, the accuracy for retrieval module is 0.96 and F1 score for deletion module is 0.85.

Comparison between two tasks. According to human evaluation results in Table 6, both BART and the pipeline received higher scores for idiomatic sentence paraphrasing than idiomatic sentence generation, suggesting that paraphrasing is relatively easier among the two tasks. This resonates with our intuitions as language users in that given a lexical resource, paraphrasing an IE is easier than finding the right IE to replace a phrase.

Limitation of automatic metrics. Table 7 presents the correlation between automatic metrics and human judgements. All the correlation scores between automatic metrics and human evaluate

scores are not high enough. For BLEU and SARI which mainly measure overlapping tokens, some synonymous idioms or literal phrases are ignored while they are still appropriate. For GRUEN metric aiming to measure text quality, its correlation scores with fluency and overall meaning are quite low. Therefore, more reliable automatic evaluation methods are needed.

Error analysis. For task of idiomatic sentence generation, the primary challenge is in identifying the appropriate IE, which is the hardest when the IE is highly non-compositional (e.g., *bird of passage* in Table 11). The examples are presented in Table 11 in the Appendix. For the task of idiomatic sentence paraphrasing, one challenge is the difficulty of choosing the correct sense of the idiom. As is shown in Table 12 in Appendix, all the baseline models were unable to generate the correct literal phrases for "alpha and omega", which have two senses: the beginning and the end; the principal element. Also, we noticed that strong baseline models of pretrained BART and the pipeline model tend to use a short but inaccurate literal phrase when the correct one is long. Paraphrasing of "the bird of passage" in Table 12 is an example.

Applications: Research in the proposed tasks has many potential practical applications. 1) An idiomatic sentence paraphrasing tool would be of importance in several language processing settings encountered by humans and machines. The non-literal and stylized meaning of multi-word expressions (MWE) in general and idioms in particular, pose two broad kinds of challenges. First, they affect readability in target populations. For in-

Corr	Context		Target		Fluency		Overall	
	s2i	i2s	s2i	i2s	s2i	i2s	s2i	i2s
BLEU	0.27	0.17	0.56	0.28	0.09	0.02	0.64	0.29
SARI	0.21	0.17	0.61	0.40	-0.02	-0.01	0.61	0.39
GRUEN	-0.18	-0.07	-0.11	0.12	0.23	0.15	-0.18	0.11

Table 7: Instance-level Spearman's correlations between human and automatic evaluation for pretrained BART.

Literal sentence		You can't **delay making a decision** any longer , you need to make up your mind .
Idiomatic sentence		You can't *sit on the fence* any longer , you need to make up your mind .
S2I	**Seq2Seq**	You can't be in the obsession any night , you need to make up your plans
	Transformer	you can't **delay making a decision** of any longer , you need to make your mind your mind .
	Seq2Seq-copy	you can't sit sit the fence any , , you need to to up your .
	Transformer-copy	you can't **delay making a decision** any longer , you need to make up your mind .
	Pipeline	You can't **delay making a decisione** any longer, you make your mind.
	BART	You can't **delay making a decision** any longer, you need to make up your own mind.
I2S	**Seq2Seq**	You can't wait on the money any rival , you need to make up your energy .
	Transformer	you can't *sit on the* ? any longer , you need to make up your mind .
	Seq2Seq-copy	you can't delay making any any any , you need to make your your mind .
	Transformer-copy	you can't *sit on the* troublesome any longer , you need to make up your mind .
	Pipeline	You can't *stay on the fence* any longer, you need to make up your mind.
	BART	You can't **be indecisive** any longer, you need to make up your mind.

Table 8: A sample of generated idiomatic sentences. Text in *bold and italics red* represents the idiomatic expressions correctly included in the outputs, text in **bold blue** represents the literal counterparts in the input sentences and text in underlined olive represents the idioms or literal phrases that are poorly generated.

stance, despite their intact structural language competence, individuals with Asperger syndrome and more broadly those with autism spectrum disorder are known to experience significant challenges understanding figurative language (idioms) in their native language (Kalandadze et al., 2018). It is also widely acknowledged that idiomatic expressions are some of the hardest aspects of language acquisition and processing for second language learners (Liontas, 2002; Ellis et al., 2008; Canut et al., 2020). Moreover, natural language processing systems are known to be negatively impacted by idioms in text ((Salton et al., 2014; Shao et al.; Shutova et al., 2013) shown the negative impact of idioms and metaphors on machine translation leading to awkward or incorrect translations from English to other languages). Fruitful results of this task can lead to a system capable of recognizing and interpreting IEs in unrestricted text in a central component of any real-world NLP application (e.g., information retrieval, machine translation, question answering, information extraction, and opinion mining).2) A realistic application of the idiomatic sentence generation task would be for computer-aided style checking, where a post-processing tool could suggest a list of idioms to replace a literal phrase in a sentence. 3) True integration with an external NLP application would require combining the first step of IE identification followed by paraphrasing as done in (Shutova et al., 2013), which will require a combination of the paraphrasing with identification, and can be a future direction for research.

7 Conclusions

To conclude, in this paper, we proposed two new tasks: idiomatic sentence generation and paraphrasing. We also presented PIE, the first parallel idiom corpus. We benchmark existing end-to-end trained neural network models and a pipeline method on PIE and analyze their performance for our tasks. Our experiments and analyses reveal the competence and shortcomings of available methods, underscoring the need for continued research on processing idiomatic expressions.

Future work should explore possibilities for improving performance through more extensive exploration of richer model architectures and using more reliable evaluation methods.

References

Keiga Abe, Kayo Sakamoto, and Masanori Nakagawa. 2006. A computational model of the metaphor generation process. In *Proceedings of the Annual Meeting of the Cognitive Science Society*, volume 28.

Sweta Agrawal and Marine Carpuat. 2020. Multitask models for controlling the complexity of neural machine translation. In *Proceedings of the The Fourth Widening Natural Language Processing Workshop*, pages 136–139.

Mona Baker. 2018. *In other words: A coursebook on translation*. Routledge.

Robert Baldwin, Martin Cave, and Martin Lodge. 2010. *The Oxford handbook of regulation*. Oxford university press.

Douglas Biber, Stig Johansson, Geoffrey Leech, Susan Conrad, and Edward Finegan. 1999. Longman grammar of written and spoken english. *Harlow: Longman.*

Emmanuelle Canut, Juliette Delahaie, and Magali Husianycia. 2020. Vous avez dit falc? pour une adaptation linguistique des textes destinés aux migrants nouvellement arrivés. *Langage et societe*, (3):171–201.

Mathieu Constant, Gülşen Eryiğit, Johanna Monti, Lonneke Van Der Plas, Carlos Ramisch, Michael Rosner, and Amalia Todirascu. 2017. Multiword expression processing: A survey. *Computational Linguistics*, 43(4):837–892.

Paul Cook, Afsaneh Fazly, and Suzanne Stevenson. 2008. The vnc-tokens dataset. In *Proceedings of the LREC Workshop Towards a Shared Task for Multiword Expressions (MWE 2008)*, pages 19–22.

Nick C Ellis, RITA Simpson-Vlach, and Carson Maynard. 2008. Formulaic language in native and second language speakers: Psycholinguistics, corpus linguistics, and tesol. *Tesol Quarterly*, 42(3):375–396.

Afsaneh Fazly, Paul Cook, and Suzanne Stevenson. 2009. Unsupervised type and token identification of idiomatic expressions. *Computational Linguistics*, 35(1):61–103.

Juri Ganitkevitch, Benjamin Van Durme, and Chris Callison-Burch. 2013. Ppdb: The paraphrase database. In *Proceedings of the 2013 Conference of the North American Chapter of the Association for Computational Linguistics: Human Language Technologies*, pages 758–764.

Sebastian Gehrmann, Yuntian Deng, and Alexander M Rush. 2018. Bottom-up abstractive summarization. *arXiv preprint arXiv:1808.10792*.

Debanjan Ghosh, Alexander R Fabbri, and Smaranda Muresan. 2018. Sarcasm analysis using conversation context. *Computational Linguistics*, 44(4):755–792.

Hongyu Gong, Suma Bhat, Lingfei Wu, JinJun Xiong, and Wen-mei Hwu. 2019. Reinforcement learning based text style transfer without parallel training corpus. In *Proceedings of the 2019 Conference of the North American Chapter of the Association for Computational Linguistics: Human Language Technologies, Volume 1 (Long and Short Papers)*, pages 3168–3180.

Yunfan Gu, Zhongyu Wei, et al. 2019. Extract, transform and filling: A pipeline model for question paraphrasing based on template. In *Proceedings of the 5th Workshop on Noisy User-generated Text (W-NUT 2019)*, pages 109–114.

Ankush Gupta, Arvind Agarwal, Prawaan Singh, and Piyush Rai. 2018. A deep generative framework for paraphrase generation. In *Thirty-Second AAAI Conference on Artificial Intelligence*.

Hessel Haagsma, Johan Bos, and Malvina Nissim. 2020. Magpie: A large corpus of potentially idiomatic expressions. In *Proceedings of The 12th Language Resources and Evaluation Conference*, pages 279–287.

Ruining He and Julian McAuley. 2016. Ups and downs: Modeling the visual evolution of fashion trends with one-class collaborative filtering. In *proceedings of the 25th international conference on world wide web*, pages 507–517.

Zhiting Hu, Zichao Yang, Xiaodan Liang, Ruslan Salakhutdinov, and Eric P Xing. 2017. Toward controlled generation of text. In *Proceedings of the 34th International Conference on Machine Learning-Volume 70*, pages 1587–1596. JMLR. org.

Julia Ive, Natalia Viani, Joyce Kam, Lucia Yin, Somain Verma, Stephen Puntis, Rudolf N Cardinal, Angus Roberts, Robert Stewart, and Sumithra Velupillai. 2020. Generation and evaluation of artificial mental health records for natural language processing. *NPJ Digital Medicine*, 3(1):1–9.

Mohit Iyyer, John Wieting, Kevin Gimpel, and Luke Zettlemoyer. 2018. Adversarial example generation with syntactically controlled paraphrase networks. In *Proceedings of the 2018 Conference of the North American Chapter of the Association for Computational Linguistics: Human Language Technologies, Volume 1 (Long Papers)*, pages 1875–1885.

Ray Jackendoff. 1995. The boundaries of the lexicon. *Idioms: Structural and psychological perspectives*, pages 133–165.

Harsh Jhamtani, Varun Gangal, Eduard Hovy, and Eric Nyberg. 2017. Shakespearizing modern language using copy-enriched sequence to sequence models. In *Proceedings of the Workshop on Stylistic Variation*, pages 10–19.

Aditya Joshi, Pushpak Bhattacharyya, and Mark J Carman. 2017. Automatic sarcasm detection: A survey. *ACM Computing Surveys (CSUR)*, 50(5):1–22.

Tamar Kalandadze, Courtenay Norbury, Terje Nærland, and Kari-Anne B Næss. 2018. Figurative language comprehension in individuals with autism spectrum disorder: A meta-analytic review. *Autism*, 22(2):99–117.

Debra Kerbel and Pam Grunwell. 1997. Idioms in the classroom: An investigation of language unit and mainstream teachers' use of idioms. *Child Language Teaching and Therapy*, 13(2):113–123.

Beata Beigman Klebanov, Kevin Knight, and Daniel Marcu. 2004. Text simplification for information-seeking applications. In *OTM Confederated International Conferences" On the Move to Meaningful Internet Systems"*, pages 735–747. Springer.

Ioannis Korkontzelos, Torsten Zesch, Fabio Massimo Zanzotto, and Chris Biemann. 2013. Semeval-2013 task 5: Evaluating phrasal semantics. In *Second Joint Conference on Lexical and Computational Semantics (* SEM), Volume 2: Proceedings of the Seventh International Workshop on Semantic Evaluation (SemEval 2013)*, pages 39–47.

Wuwei Lan, Siyu Qiu, Hua He, and Wei Xu. 2017. A continuously growing dataset of sentential paraphrases. *arXiv preprint arXiv:1708.00391*.

Alon Lavie and Abhaya Agarwal. 2007. Meteor: An automatic metric for mt evaluation with high levels of correlation with human judgments. In *Proceedings of the second workshop on statistical machine translation*, pages 228–231.

Mike Lewis, Yinhan Liu, Naman Goyal, Marjan Ghazvininejad, Abdelrahman Mohamed, Omer Levy, Ves Stoyanov, and Luke Zettlemoyer. 2019. Bart: Denoising sequence-to-sequence pre-training for natural language generation, translation, and comprehension. *arXiv preprint arXiv:1910.13461*.

Juncen Li, Robin Jia, He He, and Percy Liang. 2018. Delete, retrieve, generate: a simple approach to sentiment and style transfer. In *Proceedings of the 2018 Conference of the North American Chapter of the Association for Computational Linguistics: Human Language Technologies, Volume 1 (Long Papers)*, pages 1865–1874.

Chin-Yew Lin. 2004. ROUGE: A package for automatic evaluation of summaries. In *Text Summarization Branches Out*, pages 74–81, Barcelona, Spain. Association for Computational Linguistics.

John Liontas. 2002. Context and idiom understanding in second languages. *EUROSLA yearbook*, 2(1):155–185.

Changsheng Liu and Rebecca Hwa. 2019. A generalized idiom usage recognition model based on semantic compatibility. In *Proceedings of the AAAI Conference on Artificial Intelligence*, volume 33, pages 6738–6745.

Rui Mao, Chenghua Lin, and Frank Guerin. 2018. Word embedding and wordnet based metaphor identification and interpretation. In *Proceedings of the 56th Annual Meeting of the Association for Computational Linguistics (Volume 1: Long Papers)*, pages 1222–1231.

Julian John McAuley and Jure Leskovec. 2013. From amateurs to connoisseurs: modeling the evolution of user expertise through online reviews. In *Proceedings of the 22nd international conference on World Wide Web*, pages 897–908.

Saif Mohammad, Ekaterina Shutova, and Peter Turney. 2016. Metaphor as a medium for emotion: An empirical study. In *Proceedings of the Fifth Joint Conference on Lexical and Computational Semantics*, pages 23–33.

Smaranda Muresan, Roberto Gonzalez-Ibanez, Debanjan Ghosh, and Nina Wacholder. 2016. Identification of nonliteral language in social media: A case study on sarcasm. *Journal of the Association for Information Science and Technology*, 67(11):2725–2737.

Sergiu Nisioi, Sanja Štajner, Simone Paolo Ponzetto, and Liviu P Dinu. 2017. Exploring neural text simplification models. In *Proceedings of the 55th Annual Meeting of the Association for Computational Linguistics (Volume 2: Short Papers)*, pages 85–91.

Geoffrey Nunberg, Ivan A Sag, and Thomas Wasow. 1994. Idioms. *Language*, 70(3):491–538.

Ekaterina Ovchinnikova, Vladimir Zaytsev, Suzanne Wertheim, and Ross Israel. 2014. Generating conceptual metaphors from proposition stores. *arXiv preprint arXiv:1409.7619*.

Kishore Papineni, Salim Roukos, Todd Ward, and Wei-Jing Zhu. 2002. Bleu: a method for automatic evaluation of machine translation. In *Proceedings of the 40th annual meeting on association for computational linguistics*, pages 311–318. Association for Computational Linguistics.

Andrew Pawley and Frances Hodgetts Syder. 2014. Two puzzles for linguistic theory: Nativelike selection and nativelike fluency. In *Language and communication*, pages 203–239. Routledge.

Aaditya Prakash, Sadid A Hasan, Kathy Lee, Vivek Datla, Ashequl Qadir, Joey Liu, and Oladimeji Farri. 2016. Neural paraphrase generation with stacked residual lstm networks. In *Proceedings of COLING 2016, the 26th International Conference on Computational Linguistics: Technical Papers*, pages 2923–2934.

Sudha Rao and Joel Tetreault. 2018. Dear sir or madam, may i introduce the gyafc dataset: Corpus, benchmarks and metrics for formality style transfer. *arXiv preprint arXiv:1803.06535*.

Paul Rayson, Scott Piao, Serge Sharoff, Stefan Evert, and Begona Villada Moirón. 2010. Multiword expressions: hard going or plain sailing? *Language Resources and Evaluation*, 44(1-2):1–5.

Ivan A Sag, Timothy Baldwin, Francis Bond, Ann Copestake, and Dan Flickinger. 2002. Multiword expressions: A pain in the neck for nlp. In *International conference on intelligent text processing and computational linguistics*, pages 1–15. Springer.

Giancarlo Salton, Robert Ross, and John Kelleher. 2014. An empirical study of the impact of idioms on phrase based statistical machine translation of english to brazilian-portuguese.

Agata Savary, Carlos Ramisch, Silvio Ricardo Cordeiro, Federico Sangati, Veronika Vincze, Behrang Qasemi Zadeh, Marie Candito, Fabienne Cap, Voula Giouli, Ivelina Stoyanova, et al. 2017. The parseme shared task on automatic identification of verbal multiword expressions. In *The 13th Workshop on Multiword Expression at EACL*, pages 31–47.

Norbert Schmitt and Diane Schmitt. 2020. *Vocabulary in language teaching*. Cambridge university press.

Rico Sennrich, Barry Haddow, and Alexandra Birch. 2016. Improving neural machine translation models with monolingual data. In *Proceedings of the 54th Annual Meeting of the Association for Computational Linguistics (Volume 1: Long Papers)*, pages 86–96.

Yutong Shao, Rico Sennrich, Bonnie Webber, and Federico Fancellu. Evaluating machine translation performance on chinese idioms with a blacklist method.

Tianxiao Shen, Tao Lei, Regina Barzilay, and Tommi Jaakkola. 2017. Style transfer from non-parallel text by cross-alignment. In *Advances in neural information processing systems*, pages 6830–6841.

Ekaterina Shutova. 2010a. Automatic metaphor interpretation as a paraphrasing task. In *Human Language Technologies: The 2010 Annual Conference of the North American Chapter of the Association for Computational Linguistics*, pages 1029–1037. Association for Computational Linguistics.

Ekaterina Shutova. 2010b. Models of metaphor in nlp. In *Proceedings of the 48th annual meeting of the association for computational linguistics*, pages 688–697.

Ekaterina Shutova, Simone Teufel, and Anna Korhonen. 2013. Statistical metaphor processing. *Computational Linguistics*, 39(2):301–353.

Rita Simpson and Dushyanthi Mendis. 2003. A corpus-based study of idioms in academic speech. *Tesol Quarterly*, 37(3):419–441.

Simone A Sprenger. 2003. *Fixed expressions and the production of idioms*. Ph.D. thesis, Radboud University Nijmegen Nijmegen.

Kevin Stowe, Leonardo Ribeiro, and Iryna Gurevych. 2020. Metaphoric paraphrase generation. *arXiv preprint arXiv:2002.12854*.

Akhilesh Sudhakar, Bhargav Upadhyay, and Arjun Maheswaran. 2019. "transforming" delete, retrieve, generate approach for controlled text style transfer. In *Proceedings of the 2019 Conference on Empirical Methods in Natural Language Processing and the 9th International Joint Conference on Natural Language Processing (EMNLP-IJCNLP)*, pages 3260–3270.

Ilya Sutskever, Oriol Vinyals, and Quoc V Le. 2014. Sequence to sequence learning with neural networks. In *Advances in neural information processing systems*, pages 3104–3112.

Asuka Terai and Masanori Nakagawa. 2010. A computational system of metaphor generation with evaluation mechanism. In *International Conference on Artificial Neural Networks*, pages 142–147. Springer.

Ashish Vaswani, Noam Shazeer, Niki Parmar, Jakob Uszkoreit, Llion Jones, Aidan N Gomez, Łukasz Kaiser, and Illia Polosukhin. 2017. Attention is all you need. In *Advances in neural information processing systems*, pages 5998–6008.

John Wieting and Kevin Gimpel. 2017. Paranmt-50m: Pushing the limits of paraphrastic sentence embeddings with millions of machine translations. *arXiv preprint arXiv:1711.05732*.

Alison Wray and Michael R Perkins. 2000. The functions of formulaic language: An integrated model. *Language & Communication*, 20(1):1–28.

Sander Wubben, EJ Krahmer, and APJ van den Bosch. 2012. Sentence simplification by monolingual machine translation.

Jingjing Xu, Xu Sun, Qi Zeng, Xiaodong Zhang, Xuancheng Ren, Houfeng Wang, and Wenjie Li. 2018. Unpaired sentiment-to-sentiment translation: A cycled reinforcement learning approach. In *Proceedings of the 56th Annual Meeting of the Association for Computational Linguistics (Volume 1: Long Papers)*, pages 979–988.

Wei Xu, Chris Callison-Burch, and Courtney Napoles. 2015. Problems in current text simplification research: New data can help. *Transactions of the Association for Computational Linguistics*, 3:283–297.

Wei Xu, Courtney Napoles, Ellie Pavlick, Quanze Chen, and Chris Callison-Burch. 2016. Optimizing statistical machine translation for text simplification. *Transactions of the Association for Computational Linguistics*, 4:401–415.

Qian Yang, Dinghan Shen, Yong Cheng, Wenlin Wang, Guoyin Wang, Lawrence Carin, et al. 2019. An end-to-end generative architecture for paraphrase generation. In *Proceedings of the 2019 Conference on Empirical Methods in Natural Language Processing and the 9th International Joint Conference on Natural Language Processing (EMNLP-IJCNLP)*, pages 3123–3133.

Zhiwei Yu and Xiaojun Wan. 2019. How to avoid sentences spelling boring? towards a neural approach to unsupervised metaphor generation. In *Proceedings of the 2019 Conference of the North American Chapter of the Association for Computational Linguistics: Human Language Technologies, Volume 1 (Long and Short Papers)*, pages 861–871.

Kuo-Hao Zeng, Mohammad Shoeybi, and Ming-Yu Liu. 2020. Style example-guided text generation using generative adversarial transformers. *arXiv preprint arXiv:2003.00674*.

Xingxing Zhang and Mirella Lapata. 2017. Sentence simplification with deep reinforcement learning. *arXiv preprint arXiv:1703.10931*.

Sanqiang Zhao, Rui Meng, Daqing He, Saptono Andi, and Parmanto Bambang. 2018. Integrating transformer and paraphrase rules for sentence simplification. *arXiv preprint arXiv:1810.11193*.

Jianing Zhou, Hongyu Gong, Srihari Nanniyur, and Suma Bhat. 2021. From solving a problem boldly to cutting the gordian knot: Idiomatic text generation. *arXiv preprint arXiv:2104.06541*.

Wanzheng Zhu and Suma Bhat. 2020. Gruen for evaluating linguistic quality of generated text. In *Proceedings of the 2020 Conference on Empirical Methods in Natural Language Processing: Findings*, pages 94–108.

Zhemin Zhu, Delphine Bernhard, and Iryna Gurevych. 2010. A monolingual tree-based translation model for sentence simplification. In *Proceedings of the 23rd International Conference on Computational Linguistics (Coling 2010)*, pages 1353–1361.

A Appendix

A.1 Detailed Evaluation Results

We provide more detailed autometic evaluation results in Table 9 and 10.

A.2 Generated Examples

We provide examples generated by all models on idiomatic sentence generation and transfer tasks in Table 11 and 12 respectively.

Model	BLEU	ROUGE-1	ROUGE-2	ROUGE-L	METEOR	SARI	GRUEN	Perplexity
Seq2Seq	25.16	48.26	22.90	47.21	41.46	24.13	32.25	4.24
Seq2Seq with copy	38.02	66.11	40.37	74.04	68.21	43.02	27.79	24.43
Transformer	45.58	60.22	42.82	60.59	68.68	36.67	44.05	4.00
Transformer with copy	59.56	68.34	55.72	69.38	79.53	39.93	59.27	4.12
Pretrained BART	**79.32**	**83.95**	**77.16**	**84.20**	**83.41**	62.30	**77.49**	3.88
Pipeline	65.56	74.44	62.96	74.56	78.02	**67.64**	67.27	**3.4**

Table 9: Performance comparison of baselines for idiomatic sentence generation

Model	BLEU	ROUGE-1	ROUGE-2	ROUGE-L	METEOR	SARI	GRUEN	Perplexity
Seq2Seq	42.96	62.43	40.46	62.54	59.36	33.89	33.45	9.54
Seq2Seq with copy	47.58	71.67	50.20	76.77	77.23	49.69	32.84	21.85
Transformer	46.65	60.90	43.34	61.39	69.82	38.62	44.06	10.59
Transformer with copy	57.91	68.44	54.97	69.59	79.17	45.10	52.25	4.61
Pretrained BART	**78.53**	**84.64**	**77.21**	**84.95**	**85.36**	61.82	**78.03**	5.35
Pipeline	70.03	78.50	68.39	78.90	83.65	**62.45**	74.16	**4.25**

Table 10: Performance comparison of baselines for idiomatic sentence paraphrasing

Attribute	high non-compositionality
Literal sentence	Joe , being one who is here today and gone tomorrow , stayed the night , had some rest and ate some food and left early the next morning .
Reference	Joe , being the bird of passage he is , stayed the night , had some rest and ate some food and left early the next morning .
Seq2Seq	First , being one , and putting the project going to be joined the ones , had some ice row and creating some people and creating some expensive of both the time .
Transformer	joe , being one who is here today and gone tomorrow , kept the night , had some rest and punched some food a great early .
Seq2Seq with copy	joe , being the bird of he he , , , , , , , some some some some and and and and the .
Transformer with copy	joe , being one who is here today and gone tomorrow , stayed the night , had a rest and ate food left the next early .
Pretrained BART	Joe, being one who is here today and gone tomorrow, stayed the night, had some rest and ate some food and left early the next morning.
Pipeline	cool heels joe, being one who is here today and gone tomorrow, stayed the night, and ate some food and left early the next morning.
Attribute	**multiple meaning**
Literal sentence	My life starts from you and ends at you , so you are my first and my last .
Reference	My life starts from you and ends at you , so you are my alpha and omega .
Seq2Seq	My friend from you and offensive , and yet you are my dream and my loved .
Transformer	my life starts from you and anything at you , so you are my first sight and my last .
Seq2Seq with copy	my life starts from you and at you you you you you you my my and .
Transformer with copy	My life starts from you and ends at you , so you are my first and my last .
Pretrained BART	My life starts from you and ends at you , so you are my first and my last.
Pipeline	Close the books, so you are my my first and my last.
Attribute	**high non-compositionality**
Literal sentence	You can't delay making a decision any longer , you need to make up your mind .
Reference	You can't sit on the fence any longer , you need to make up your mind .
Seq2Seq	You can't be in the obsession any night , you need to make up your plans .
Transformer	you can't delay making a decision of any longer , you need to make your mind your mind .
Seq2Seq with copy	you can't sit sit the fence any , , you need to to up your .
Transformer with copy	you can't delay making a decision any longer , you need to make up your mind .
Pretrained BART	You can't delay making a decision any longer, you need to make up your own mind.
Pipeline	You can't delay making a decisione any longer, you make your mind.
Attribute	**low non-compositionality**
Literal sentence	Finding the ruins of Babylon was the archaeologist 's greatest find .
Reference	Finding the ruins of Babylon was the archaeologist 's treasure trove .
Seq2Seq	Missing the aftermath of pouring down the cake 's share of the city .
Transformer	catching up with silver lining of the challenges 's volatility .
Seq2Seq with copy	finding the ruins of unk was the 's 's trove .
Transformer with copy	finding the ruins of babylon was the archaeologist 's greatest silver spoons .
Pretrained BART	Finding the ruins of Babylon was the archaeologist's greatest find.
Pipeline	Finding the ruins of babylon was the archaeologist' treasure trove.

Table 11: Samples of generated idiomatic sentences. Text in blue represents the idiomatic expressions correctly included in the outputs; text in red represents the literal counterparts in the input sentences. text in green represents the idioms that are poorly generated.

Attribute	high non-compositionality
Idiomatic sentence	Joe , being the bird of passage he is , stayed the night , had some rest and ate some food and left early the next morning .
Reference	Joe , being one who is here today and gone tomorrow , stayed the night , had some rest and ate some food and left early the next morning .
Seq2Seq	And , sitting the part of the Bieber he is , seemed the morning , he some smart and wound problems so well and gives early at the next morning .
Transformer	joe , being the guards of nowhere he is , the night the night , and had some dealers and left the morning left the next morning .
Seq2Seq with copy	joe , being one who here today and tomorrow tomorrow stayed stayed night , had some and and and and and left next next next .
Transformer with copy	joe , being the bird of energy is stayed , stayed the night , some rest and ate ate some food left the next morning .
Pretrained BART	Joe, being the traveler he is, stayed the night, had some rest and ate some food and left early the next morning.
Pipeline	joe, being the person he is, stayed the night, had some rest and ate some food and left early the next morning.

Attribute	multiple meaning
Idiomatic sentence	My life starts from you and ends with you , so you are my alpha and omega .
Reference	My life starts from you and ends with you , so you are my first and my last .
Seq2Seq	My life dreams from you and read your family at you , so you are .
Transformer	my life starts from you and learn at you , so you are my most important part .
Seq2Seq with copy	my life starts from you ends ends you , so you my my my my last last last .
Transformer with copy	my life starts from you and ends with you , so you are my wish and omega .
Pretrained BART	My life starts from you and ends with you, so you are my most important part.
Pipeline	My life starts from you and ends with you, so you are my most important part.

Attribute	high non-compositionality
Idiomatic sentence	You can't sit on the fence any longer , you need to make up your mind .
Reference	You can't delay making a decision any longer , you need to make up your mind .
Seq2Seq	You can't wait on the money any rival , you need to make up your energy .
Transformer	you can't sit on the ? any longer , you need to make up your mind .
Seq2Seq with copy	you can't delay making any any any , you need to make your your mind .
Transformer with copy	you ca n't sit on the troublesome any longer , you need to make your mind .
Pretrained BART	You can't be indecisive any longer, you need to make up your mind.
Pipeline	You can't stay on the fence any longer, you need to make up your mind.

Attribute	low non-compositionality
Idiomatic sentence	Finding the ruins of Babylon was the archaeologist 's treasure trove .
Reference	Finding the ruins of Babylon was the archaeologist 's greatest find .
Seq2Seq	Edward the trap of nature was the racial out of Robert .
Transformer	finding and hide of confiement was shocking 's legal code .
Seq2Seq with copy	finding the ruins of unk was the unk 's greatest find .
Transformer with copy	finding the ruins of babylon was the archaeologist's family members .
Pretrained BART	Finding the ruins of Babylon was the archaeologist's greatest find.
Pipeline	Finding the ruins of babylon was the archaeologist's trove.

Table 12: Samples of generated literal sentences. Text in red represents the appropriate literal phrases included in the outputs. Text in blue represents the idioms in the input sentences. Text in green represents the literal phrases that are poorly generated.

Lexical Semantic Recognition

Nelson F. Liu
Stanford University
nfliu@cs.stanford.edu

Daniel Hershcovich
University of Copenhagen
dh@di.ku.dk

Michael Kranzlein   Nathan Schneider
Georgetown University
{mmk119, nathan.schneider}@georgetown.edu

Abstract

In lexical semantics, full-sentence segmentation and segment labeling of various phenomena are generally treated separately, despite their interdependence. We hypothesize that a unified *lexical semantic recognition* task is an effective way to encapsulate previously disparate styles of annotation, including multiword expression identification/classification and supersense tagging. Using the STREUSLE corpus, we train a neural CRF sequence tagger and evaluate its performance along various axes of annotation. As the label set generalizes that of previous tasks (PARSEME, DiMSUM), we additionally evaluate how well the model generalizes to those test sets, finding that it approaches or surpasses existing models despite training only on STREUSLE. Our work also establishes baseline models and evaluation metrics for integrated and accurate modeling of lexical semantics, facilitating future work in this area.

1 Introduction

Many NLP tasks traditionally approached as tagging focus on lexical semantic behavior—they aim to identify and categorize lexical semantic units in running text using a general set of labels. Two examples are supersense tagging of nouns and verbs as formulated by Ciaramita and Altun (2006), and verbal multiword expression (MWE) identification and classification in the multilingual PARSEME shared tasks (Savary et al., 2017; Ramisch et al., 2018, 2020). By analogy with named entity recognition, we can use the term **lexical semantic recognition** (LSR) for such chunking-and-labeling tasks that apply to lexical meaning generally, not just entities. This disambiguation can serve as a foundational layer of analysis for downstream applications in natural language processing, and provides an initial level of organization for compiling lexical resources, such as semantic nets and thesauri.

In this paper, we tackle a more inclusive LSR task of lexical semantic segmentation and disambiguation. The STREUSLE corpus (see §2) contains comprehensive annotations of MWEs (along with their holistic syntactic status) and noun, verb, and preposition/possessive supersenses. We train a neural CRF tagger (Lafferty et al., 2001) using BERT embeddings (Devlin et al., 2019) and find that it obtains strong results as a first baseline for this task in its full form.

In addition, we ask: Does a tagger trained on STREUSLE generalize to evaluations like the PARSEME shared task on verbal MWEs (Ramisch et al., 2018) and the DiMSUM shared task on MWEs and noun/verb supersenses (Schneider et al., 2016)? Results show our LSR model based on STREUSLE is general enough to capture different types of analysis consistently, and suggest an integrated full-sentence tagging framework is valuable for explicit modeling of lexical semantics in NLP.[1]

2 LSR Tagging Frameworks

Our tagger is based on STREUSLE (Supersense-Tagged Repository of English with a Unified Semantics for Lexical Expressions; Schneider and Smith, 2015; Schneider et al., 2018),[2] a corpus of web reviews annotated comprehensively for lexical semantic units and supersense labels. Specifically, there are three annotation layers: **multiword expressions**, **lexical categories**, and **supersenses**. The supersenses apply to noun, verb, and prepositional/possessive units. Figure 1 shows an example.

Many of the component annotations have been applied to other languages: verbal multiword expressions (Savary et al., 2017; Ramisch et al., 2018), noun and verb supersenses (e.g., Picca et al.,

---

[1]Code, pretrained models, and model and scorer output (all train/dev/test splits) can be found at https://nelsonliu.me/papers/lexical-semantic-recognition

[2]https://github.com/nert-nlp/streusle

Proceedings of the 17th Workshop on Multiword Expressions, pages 49–56
Bangkok, Thailand (online), August 6, 2021. ©2021 Association for Computational Linguistics

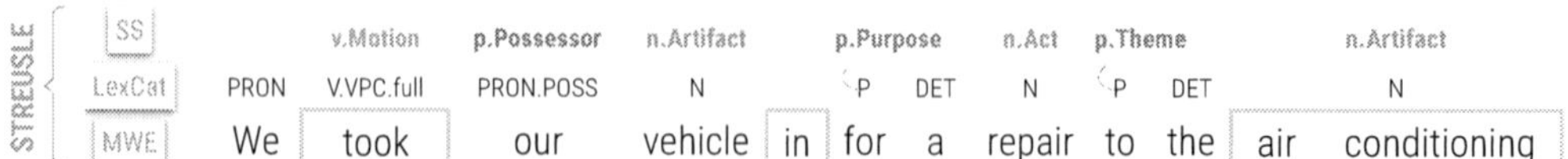

Figure 1: Example annotated sentence from the STREUSLE training set. The (strong) multiword expressions "took... in" and "air conditioning" each receive a single lexcat and supersense. UD syntax is not shown.

2008; Qiu et al., 2011; Schneider et al., 2013; Martínez Alonso et al., 2015; Hellwig, 2017), and adposition supersenses (Hwang et al., 2017; Zhu et al., 2019). In this paper we focus on English, where comprehensive annotation is available.

2.1 STREUSLE Annotation Layers

STREUSLE comprises the entire 55K-word Reviews section of the English Web Treebank (Bies et al., 2012), for which there are gold Universal Dependencies (UD; Nivre et al., 2020) graphs, and adopts the same train/dev/test split.

The lexical-level annotations do not make use of the UD parse directly, but there are constraints on compatibility between lexical categories and UPOS tags (see §3).

Multiword expressions (MWEs; Baldwin and Kim, 2010) are expressed as groupings of two or more tokens into idiomatic or collocational units. As detailed by Schneider et al. (2014a,b), these units may be contiguous or *gappy* (discontinuous).[3] Each unit is marked with a binary *strength* value: idiomatic/noncompositional expressions are *strong*; collocations that are nevertheless semantically compositional, like "highly recommended", are *weak*.

We use the term **lexical unit** for any expression that is either a *strong* MWE grouping of multiple tokens, or a token that does not belong to a strong MWE. Every token in the sentence thus belongs to exactly one lexical unit. The other layers of semantic annotation augment lexical units, and weak MWEs are groupings of (entire) lexical units.

Lexical categories (lexcats) describe the syntax of lexical units. They are similar to UPOS tags available in the UD annotations of the corpus, but are necessary in order to (a) express refinements relevant to the criteria for the application of supersenses, and (b) account for the overall syntactic behavior of strong MWEs, which may not be obvious from their internal syntactic structure.[4] Appendix A gives the full list of lexcats.

Supersenses semantically classify lexical units and provide a measure of disambiguation in context. There are 3 sets of supersense labels: nominal, verbal, and prepositional/possessive. The lexcat determines which of these sets (if any) should apply.[5]

The MWE, lexcat, and supersense information over lexical units is serialized as per-token tags in a BIO-based encoding (details in §2.1.1).

2.1.1 Tag Serialization

STREUSLE specifies **token-level tags** to allow modeling lexical semantic recognition as sequence tagging. The `BbIiOo_~` tagging scheme (Schneider et al., 2014a) consists of 8 positional flags indicating MWE status: `O` applies to single-word expressions, `B` to the start of a new MWE, `I_` to the continuation of a strong MWE, and `I~` to the continuation of a weak MWE (if not continuing a strong MWE within the weak MWE). The lowercase counterparts `o`, `b`, `i_`, `i~` are the same except they are used within the gap of a discontinuous MWE. For MWE identification, local constraints on tag bigrams—e.g., that the bigrams ⟨B,B⟩ and ⟨B,O⟩ are invalid, and that the sentence must end with `I_`, `I~`, or `O`—ensure a valid overall segmentation into units (Schneider and Smith, 2015).

The lexcat and (where applicable) supersense information is incorporated in the *first* tag of each lexical unit.[6] Thus `B-N-n.ARTIFACT` indicates the

---

[3]The gap in a discontinuous MWE may contain single-word and/or other multiword expressions, provided that those embedded MWEs do not themselves contain gaps.

[4]This is also done in other resources (e.g., Shigeto et al., 2013; Gerdes et al., 2018).

[5]Some preposition units are labeled with two supersenses drawn from the same label set: the **scene role** label represents the semantic role of the prepositional *phrase* marked by the preposition, and **function** label represents the lexical contribution of the *preposition* in itself (Schneider et al., 2018). The scene role and the function are identical by default.

[6]Though in named entity recognition it is typical to include the class label on every token in the multiword unit, STREUSLE does not do this because it would create a nonlocal constraint across gaps (that the tags at either end have matching lexcat and supersense information). A tagger would either need to use a more expensive decoding algorithm or would need to greatly enhance the state space so within-gap tags capture information about the gappy expression.

In STREUSLE there is actually a slight limitation due to the verbal lexcats, which distinguish between single-word and strong multiword expressions (see Appendix A): if a `B-*` or `I~-*` tag is followed by a gap, there is no local indication of whether the expression will be strong or weak (strength is indicated only after the gap). If the expression being started is strong, then one of the verbal MWE subtypes (`V.VID`, etc.)

beginning of an MWE whose lexcat is `N` and supersense is `N.ARTIFACT`. `I_` and `i_` tags never contain lexcat or supersense information as they continue a lexical unit, whereas `O`, `B`, `I~`, `o`, `b`, and `i~` always do. Figure 2 illustrates the full tagging. All told, STREUSLE has 601 complete tags.

```
We/O-PRON          took/B-V.VPC.full-v.Motion
our/o-PRON.POSS  vehicle/o-N-n.ARTIFACT  in/I_
for/O-P-p.Purpose   a/O-DET   repair/O-N-n.ACT
to/O-P-p.Theme   the/O-DET   air/B-N-n.ARTIFACT
conditioning/I_
```

Figure 2: Serialization as token-level tags for the example sentence from figure 1.

2.2 Related Frameworks

The Universal Semantic Tagset takes a similar approach (Bjerva et al., 2016; Abzianidze and Bos, 2017; Abdou et al., 2018), and defines a cross-linguistic inventory of semantic classes for content and function words, which is designed as a substrate for compositional semantics, and does not have a trivial mapping to STREUSLE categories.

However, two shared task datasets consist of subsets of the categories used for STREUSLE annotations, on text from different sources.

PARSEME Verbal MWEs. The first such dataset is the English test set for the PARSEME 1.1 Shared Task (Ramisch et al., 2018), which covers several genres (including literature and several web genres) and is annotated only for verbal multiword expressions. The STREUSLE lexcats for verbal MWEs are identical to those of PARSEME; thus, a tagger that predicts full STREUSLE-style annotations can be evaluated for verbal MWE identification and subtyping by simply discarding the supersenses and the non-verbal MWEs and lexcats from the output.

DiMSUM. The second shared task dataset is DiMSUM (Schneider et al., 2016), which was annotated in three genres—TrustPilot web reviews, TED talk transcripts, and tweets—echoing the annotation style of STREUSLE when it contained only MWEs and noun and verb supersenses. DiMSUM does not contain prepositional/possessive supersenses or lexcats. It also lacks weak MWEs.

3 Modeling

We develop and evaluate a strong neural sequence tagger on the full task of lexical semantic recognition with MWEs and noun/verb/preposition/possessive supersenses to assess the performance of modern techniques on the full joint tagging task. Our tagger feeds pre-trained BERT representations (Devlin et al., 2019) through a biLSTM. An affine transformation followed by a linear chain conditional random field produces the final output. For further implementation details, see Appendix B.

The predicted tag for each token is the conjunction of its MWE, lexcat, and supersense.[7] There are 572 such tags in the STREUSLE training set, and only 12 unique conjoined tags in the development set are unseen during training ($\approx$5% of the development set tagging space, corresponding to $\approx$0.2% of the tokens in the development set).

Constrained Decoding. A few hard constraints are imposed in tagging. To enforce valid *MWE chunks*, we use first-order Viterbi decoding with the appropriate corpus-specific constraints (e.g., for STREUSLE MWEs, the `BbIiOo_~` tagset; see §2.1.1). The MWE constraint is applied during training and evaluation. In addition, a given token's possible lexcats are constrained by the token's *POS tag and lemma*. For instance, a token with the `AUX` UPOS tag can only take the `AUX` lexcat. However, if the token's UPOS is `AUX` and its lemma is "be", it can take either the `AUX` or `V` lexcats.

The POS and lemma constraints are only applied during evaluation; to avoid relying on gold POS/lemma annotations at test time we use an off-the-shelf system (Qi et al., 2018).

3.1 Experiments

We train the tagger on version 4.3 of the English STREUSLE corpus and evaluate on the STREUSLE, English PARSEME, and DiMSUM test sets (§2). The latter two are (zero-shot) out-of-domain test sets; the tagger is not retrained on the associated shared task training data.

We also compare to a model with static word representations by replacing BERT with the concatenation of 300-dimensional pretrained GloVe embeddings (Pennington et al., 2014) and the output of a character-level convolutional neural net-

---

should apply; whereas the correct lexcat for a single-word verb is plain `V`. In practice this is not a problem.

[7]For prepositions and possessives, the supersense is either a pair of labels, or a single label serving dually as scene role and function (fn. 5).

STREUSLE 4.3 (test, 5,381 words)	Tags			NOUN	VERB	SNACS			MWE LinkAvg			VERB MWE ID
	Full Accuracy	−LC	−SS	Labeled F	Labeled F	Labeled F	Role F	Fxn F	P	R	F	F
# Gold	5381			986	697	485			433.5			66
BERT GloVe (Gold)	82.5 79.3	82.7	89.9	69.0 66.1	77.1 72.1	71.4 61.0	72.4	81.7	80.0	64.9	71.6 59.5	63.9 38.6
BERT GloVe (Pred.)	81.0 77.5	81.7	87.9	68.0 65.7	75.1 70.0	71.6 58.0	72.4	82.8	77.6	63.1	69.5 60.3	62.3 43.0
BERT GloVe (None)	82.0 77.1	82.7	89.1	69.6 64.9	76.8 70.3	70.9 58.1	71.9	81.0	82.0	64.3	72.0 60.3	63.9 42.5
Schneider et al.	−	−	−	−	−	55.7	58.2	66.7	−	−	−	−

Table 1: STREUSLE test set results (%). (Gold): gold POS/lemmas (used in constraints only). (Pred.): predicted POS/lemmas. (None): MWE constraints only. −LC: excluding lexical category. −SS: excluding supersense. Labeled F: labeled identification F_1-score. SNACS: preposition supersenses. MWE LinkAvg P, R, F: evaluates MWE identification with partial credit. Identification of verbal MWEs (exact match) is equivalent to the PARSEME MWE-based metric. Schneider et al. (2018): previous best full SNACS tagger, reported on STREUSLE 4.0.

PARSEME 1.1 (EN-test, 71,002 words) — DiMSUM 1.0 (test, 16,500 words)

MWE-based			Token-based				MWEs			Supersenses			Combined			
P	R	F	P	R	F		P	R	F	P	R	F	Acc	P	R	F
501			1087			# Gold	1115			4745			5860			
36.1	45.5	40.3	40.2	52.0	45.4	BERT (Gold)	47.9	52.2	50.0	52.1	56.5	54.2	76.9	51.3	55.7	53.4
34.1	45.9	39.2	37.1	52.2	43.4	BERT (Pred.)	48.8	50.7	49.7	49.1	53.9	51.4	75.1	49.1	53.3	51.1
36.2	45.3	40.3	40.4	51.8	45.4	BERT (None)	53.0	49.2	51.0	50.8	55.1	52.9	76.5	51.2	53.9	52.5
33.8	32.7	33.3	37.3	31.8	34.4	Nerima+ Kirilin+	73.5	48.4	58.4	56.8	59.2	58.0	85.3	59.0	57.2	58.1
−	−	36.0	−	−	40.2	Taslimipoor+										
−	−	41.9	−	−	−	Rohanian+										

Table 2: PARSEME and DiMSUM zero-shot test set results (%) for BERT models from table 1, compared to prior published results on the tasks. GloVe F1 scores (not shown) are 17–20 points below the corresponding BERT scores for PARSEME, and 14–15 for DiMSUM. Kirilin et al. (2016): the best performing system from Schneider et al. (2016). Kirilin et al. (2016) and other shared task systems had access to gold POS/lemmas and Twitter training data in addition to all of STREUSLE for training. Nerima et al. (2017): a rule-based system which performed best for English in the shared task (Ramisch et al., 2018). Taslimipoor et al. (2019), Rohanian et al. (2019): more recent results on the test set (both used ELMo and dependency parses; only some scores were reported).

work. Finally, we also establish an upper bound on performance by providing the model with gold POS tags and lemmas; note that the difference between gold and predicted POS tags and lemmas only applies to the constrained decoding.

3.2 Results and Discussion

Table 1 shows all standard **STREUSLE** evaluation metrics on the test set. For preposition supersenses (SNACS), we compare to the results in Schneider et al. (2018), who performed MWE identification and supersense labeling for prepositions only. Note that Schneider et al. (2018) used version 4.0 of the STREUSLE corpus, which is slightly different from the version we use (some of the SNACS annotations have been revised). However, our baseline tagger, even with GloVe embeddings, outperforms Schneider et al. (2018) on that subset. Using BERT embeddings with constraints POS tags and lemmas improves performance substantially; on preposition supersense tagging, it even outperforms using gold POS tags and lemmas. Liu et al. (2019) also found that BERT embeddings improved SNACS labeling on STREUSLE 4.0, although they study a simplified setting (gold preposition identification,

and only considering single words).

Table 2 shows standard **PARSEME** and **DiMSUM** test set evaluation metrics, for models trained on the STREUSLE training set, in a zero-shot out-of-domain evaluation setting. On the PARSEME test set, our BERT-based model approaches the state-of-the-art MWE-based F-score and exceeds the best reported *fully-supervised* token-based F-score. However, on the DiMSUM test set, the BERT model did not outperform the best shared task system, likely owing to the comparative difficulty of the full lexical semantic recognition task versus the restricted DiMSUM setting.

These results demonstrate that pre-training contextualized embeddings on large corpora can help models generalize to out-of-domain settings.[8]

Constrained decoding does not substantially impact the performance of our BERT model. In general, constraints with gold POS/lemmas perform the best, while not using POS/lemma constraints is

---

[8] A small fraction of sentences in the PARSEME test set (194/3965) are EWT reviews sentences that also appear in STREUSLE's dev set. The rest of the PARSEME test set contains other web and non-web genres (Walsh et al., 2018), and thus it is mostly out-of-domain relative to STREUSLE. None of the PARSEME training set overlaps with STREUSLE.

I   have   a   new   born daughter   and   she   helped   me   with   a   lot
O-PRON O-V-v.stative O-DET O-ADJ I_   O-N-n.PERSON O-CCONJ O-PRON O-V-v.social o-PRON O-P-p.Theme B-DET I_
O-PRON O-V-v.stative O-DET B-ADJ I_   O-N-n.PERSON O-CCONJ O-PRON O-V-v.social O-PRON O-P-p.Theme B-DET I_

Go   down   1   block   to   Super   8   .
B-V.VPC.semi-v.motion I_   O-NUM O-N-n.COGNITION O-P-p.Goal B-N-n.LOCATION O-NUM O-PUNCT
O-V-v.motion   O-P-p.Direction O-NUM O-N-n.LOCATION O-P-p.Goal B-N-n.LOCATION I_   O-PUNCT
O-V-v.motion   O-P-p.Direction O-NUM O-N-n.RELATION O-P-p.Goal B-N-n.GROUP   I_   O-PUNCT

beware   they   will   rip   u   off
O-V-v.cognition O-PRON O-AUX O-V-v.contact   o-PRON I_
O-V-v.cognition O-PRON O-AUX B-V.VPC.full-v.social o-PRON I_

Figure 3: Selected examples where the model without MWE constraints (first row under each sentence) produces a structurally invalid tagging. Incorrect tags are red; the ones that render the tagging structurally invalid are bold. The last row under each sentence is the gold annotation, and the middle row (if different from gold) is the model prediction with MWE constraints. (The first sentence ends with a period, omitted for brevity.)

often better than using predicted POS/lemmas. Removing the MWE constraints yields models with slightly higher overall tag accuracy, but results in invalid segmentations for a large proportion of sentences: 14% of STREUSLE sentences in the fully unconstrained model and 17% of sentences if only predicted POS and lemmas are used for constraints.

Three sentences out of those 17% appear in figure 3. The first shows both an omission of a "B-" tag needed to start an MWE ("new") and a false positive gap without members of an MWE on either side ("me"). When the full set of constraints is used, the gold tagging is recovered. In the second sentence, there is a false positive yet structurally valid MWE ("Go down") as well as an invalid start to an MWE that is never continued ("Super"), perhaps because it is rare for a number to continue an MWE (this happens <20 times in the entire corpus). Finally, in the third sentence, the model constrained only by POS and lemma is inclined toward the literal meaning of "rip", whereas the MWE-constrained model recovers the gappy verb-particle construction "rip off". Naturally, in other sentences, the MWE-constrained model sometimes suffers from false positive or false negative MWEs, but always produces a coherent segmentation.

4   Related Work

The computational study of MWEs has a long history (Sag et al., 2002; Diab and Bhutada, 2009; Baldwin and Kim, 2010; Ramisch, 2015; Qu et al., 2015; Constant et al., 2017; Bingel and Søgaard, 2017; Shwartz and Dagan, 2019), as does supersense tagging (Segond et al., 1997; Ciaramita and Altun, 2006). Vincze et al. (2011) developed a sequence tagger for both MWEs and named entities in English. Schneider and Smith (2015); Schneider et al. (2016) featured joint tagging of MWEs and noun and verb supersenses with feature-based sequence models. Richardson (2017) trained such a model on STREUSLE 3.0 as a noun, verb, and preposition supersense tagger (without modeling MWEs). For preposition supersenses, Gonen and Goldberg (2016) incorporated multilingual cues; Schneider et al. (2018) experimented with feature-based and neural classifiers; and Liu et al. (2019), modeling supersense disambiguation of single-word prepositions only, found pretretrained contextual embeddings to be much more effective even with simple linear probing models.

5   Conclusion

We study the lexical semantic recognition task defined by the STREUSLE corpus, which involves joint MWE identification and coarse-grained (supersense) disambiguation of noun, verb, and preposition expressions; this task subsumes and unifies the previous PARSEME and DiMSUM evaluations. We develop a strong baseline neural sequence model, and see encouraging results on the task. Furthermore, zero-shot out-of-domain evaluation of our baselines on partial versions of the task yields scores comparable to the fully-supervised in-domain state of the art.

Acknowledgments

We are grateful to anonymous reviewers as well as members of the NERT lab for their feedback on this work. This research was supported in part by NSF award IIS-1812778 and grant 2016375 from the United States–Israel Binational Science Foundation (BSF), Jerusalem, Israel. NL is supported by an NSF Graduate Research Fellowship under grant number DGE-1656518.

References

Mostafa Abdou, Artur Kulmizev, Vinit Ravishankar, Lasha Abzianidze, and Johan Bos. 2018. What can we learn from semantic tagging? In *Proc. of EMNLP*, pages 4881–4889, Brussels, Belgium.

Lasha Abzianidze and Johan Bos. 2017. Towards universal semantic tagging. In *Proc. of IWCS*, Montpellier, France.

Timothy Baldwin and Su Nam Kim. 2010. Multiword expressions. In Nitin Indurkhya and Fred J. Damerau, editors, *Handbook of Natural Language Processing, Second Edition*, pages 267–292. CRC Press, Taylor and Francis Group, Boca Raton, FL.

Ann Bies, Justin Mott, Colin Warner, and Seth Kulick. 2012. English Web Treebank. Technical Report LDC2012T13, Linguistic Data Consortium, Philadelphia, PA.

Joachim Bingel and Anders Søgaard. 2017. Identifying beneficial task relations for multi-task learning in deep neural networks. In *Proc. of EACL*, pages 164–169, Valencia, Spain.

Johannes Bjerva, Barbara Plank, and Johan Bos. 2016. Semantic tagging with deep residual networks. In *Proc. of COLING*, pages 3531–3541, Osaka, Japan.

Massimiliano Ciaramita and Yasemin Altun. 2006. Broad-coverage sense disambiguation and information extraction with a supersense sequence tagger. In *Proc. of EMNLP*, pages 594–602, Sydney, Australia.

Mathieu Constant, Gülşen Eryiğit, Johanna Monti, Lonneke van der Plas, Carlos Ramisch, Michael Rosner, and Amalia Todirascu. 2017. Multiword expression processing: a survey. *Computational Linguistics*, 43(4):837–892.

Jacob Devlin, Ming-Wei Chang, Kenton Lee, and Kristina Toutanova. 2019. BERT: Pre-training of deep bidirectional transformers for language understanding. In *Proc. of NAACL-HLT*, pages 4171–4186, Minneapolis, Minnesota.

Mona Diab and Pravin Bhutada. 2009. Verb noun construction MWE token classification. In *Proc. of MWE*, pages 17–22, Suntec, Singapore.

Kim Gerdes, Bruno Guillaume, Sylvain Kahane, and Guy Perrier. 2018. SUD or surface-syntactic universal dependencies: An annotation scheme near-isomorphic to UD. In *Proceedings of the Second Workshop on Universal Dependencies (UDW 2018)*, pages 66–74, Brussels, Belgium. Association for Computational Linguistics.

Hila Gonen and Yoav Goldberg. 2016. Semi supervised preposition-sense disambiguation using multilingual data. In *Proc. of COLING*, pages 2718–2729, Osaka, Japan.

Oliver Hellwig. 2017. Coarse semantic classification of rare nouns using cross-lingual data and recurrent neural networks. In *Proc. of IWCS*, Montpellier, France.

Jena D. Hwang, Archna Bhatia, Na-Rae Han, Tim O'Gorman, Vivek Srikumar, and Nathan Schneider. 2017. Double trouble: the problem of construal in semantic annotation of adpositions. In *Proc. of *SEM*, pages 178–188, Vancouver, Canada.

Angelika Kirilin, Felix Krauss, and Yannick Versley. 2016. ICL-HD at SemEval-2016 Task 10: Improving the Detection of Minimal Semantic Units and their Meanings with an ontology and word embeddings. In *Proc. of SemEval*, pages 937–945, San Diego, California.

John D. Lafferty, Andrew McCallum, and Fernando C. N. Pereira. 2001. Conditional random fields: probabilistic models for segmenting and labeling sequence data. In *Proc. of ICML*, pages 282–289, Williamstown, MA, USA.

Nelson F. Liu, Matt Gardner, Yonatan Belinkov, Matthew E. Peters, and Noah A. Smith. 2019. Linguistic knowledge and transferability of contextual representations. In *Proc. of NAACL-HLT*, pages 1073–1094, Minneapolis, Minnesota.

Héctor Martínez Alonso, Anders Johannsen, Sussi Olsen, Sanni Nimb, Nicolai Hartvig Sørensen, Anna Braasch, Anders Søgaard, and Bolette Sandford Pedersen. 2015. Supersense tagging for Danish. In *Proc. of NODALIDA*, pages 21–29, Vilnius, Lithuania.

Luka Nerima, Vasiliki Foufi, and Éric Wehrli. 2017. Parsing and MWE detection: Fips at the PARSEME shared task. In *Proceedings of the 13th Workshop on Multiword Expressions (MWE 2017)*, pages 54–59, Valencia, Spain. Association for Computational Linguistics.

Joakim Nivre, Marie-Catherine de Marneffe, Filip Ginter, Jan Hajič, Christopher D. Manning, Sampo Pyysalo, Sebastian Schuster, Francis Tyers, and Daniel Zeman. 2020. Universal Dependencies v2: An evergrowing multilingual treebank collection. In *Proc. of LREC*, pages 4027–4036, Marseille, France.

Jeffrey Pennington, Richard Socher, and Christopher Manning. 2014. GloVe: Global vectors for word representation. In *Proc. of EMNLP*, pages 1532–1543, Doha, Qatar.

Davide Picca, Alfio Massimiliano Gliozzo, and Massimiliano Ciaramita. 2008. Supersense Tagger for Italian. In *Proc. of LREC*, pages 2386–2390, Marrakech, Morocco.

Peng Qi, Timothy Dozat, Yuhao Zhang, and Christopher D. Manning. 2018. Universal Dependency parsing from scratch. In *Proc. of CoNLL*, pages 160–170, Brussels, Belgium.

Likun Qiu, Yunfang Wu, Yanqiu Shao, and Alexander Gelbukh. 2011. Combining contextual and structural information for supersense tagging of Chinese unknown words. In *Computational Linguistics and Intelligent Text Processing: Proceedings of the 12th International Conference (CICLing'11)*, volume 6608 of *Lecture Notes in Computer Science*, pages 15–28. Springer, Berlin.

Lizhen Qu, Gabriela Ferraro, Liyuan Zhou, Weiwei Hou, Nathan Schneider, and Timothy Baldwin. 2015. Big data small data, in domain out-of domain, known word unknown word: the impact of word representations on sequence labelling tasks. In *Proc. of CoNLL*, pages 83–93, Beijing, China.

Carlos Ramisch. 2015. Multiword expressions acquisition. *A Generic and Open Framework. Cham: Springer International Publishing.*

Carlos Ramisch, Silvio Ricardo Cordeiro, Agata Savary, Veronika Vincze, Verginica Barbu Mititelu, Archna Bhatia, Maja Buljan, Marie Candito, Polona Gantar, Voula Giouli, Tunga Güngör, Abdelati Hawwari, Uxoa Iñurrieta, Jolanta Kovalevskaitė, Simon Krek, Timm Lichte, Chaya Liebeskind, Johanna Monti, Carla Parra Escartín, Behrang QasemiZadeh, Renata Ramisch, Nathan Schneider, Ivelina Stoyanova, Ashwini Vaidya, and Abigail Walsh. 2018. Edition 1.1 of the PARSEME Shared Task on Automatic Identification of Verbal Multiword Expressions. In *Proc. of LAW-MWE-CxG-2018*, pages 222–240, Santa Fe, New Mexico, USA.

Carlos Ramisch, Agata Savary, Bruno Guillaume, Jakub Waszczuk, Marie Candito, Ashwini Vaidya, Verginica Barbu Mititelu, Archna Bhatia, Uxoa Iñurrieta, Voula Giouli, Tunga Güngör, Menghan Jiang, Timm Lichte, Chaya Liebeskind, Johanna Monti, Renata Ramisch, Sara Stymne, Abigail Walsh, and Hongzhi Xu. 2020. Edition 1.2 of the PARSEME shared task on semi-supervised identification of verbal multiword expressions. In *Proceedings of the Joint Workshop on Multiword Expressions and Electronic Lexicons*, pages 107–118, online. Association for Computational Linguistics.

Oliver Ethan Richardson. 2017. *Joint prediction of supersense relations.* Bachelor's thesis, University of Utah, Salt Lake City, Utah.

Omid Rohanian, Shiva Taslimipoor, Samaneh Kouchaki, Le An Ha, and Ruslan Mitkov. 2019. Bridging the gap: Attending to discontinuity in identification of multiword expressions. In *Proc. of NAACL-HLT*, pages 2692–2698, Minneapolis, Minnesota.

Ivan Sag, Timothy Baldwin, Francis Bond, Ann Copestake, and Dan Flickinger. 2002. Multiword expressions: a pain in the neck for NLP. In Alexander Gelbukh, editor, *Computational Linguistics and Intelligent Text Processing*, volume 2276 of *Lecture Notes in Computer Science*, pages 189–206. Springer, Berlin.

Agata Savary, Carlos Ramisch, Silvio Ricardo Cordeiro, Federico Sangati, Veronika Vincze, Behrang QasemiZadeh, Marie Candito, Fabienne Cap, Voula Giouli, Ivelina Stoyanova, and Antoine Doucet. 2017. The PARSEME Shared Task on Automatic Identification of Verbal Multiword Expressions. In *Proc. of the 13th Workshop on Multiword Expressions (MWE 2017)*, pages 31–47, Valencia, Spain.

Nathan Schneider, Emily Danchik, Chris Dyer, and Noah A. Smith. 2014a. Discriminative lexical semantic segmentation with gaps: running the MWE gamut. *Transactions of the Association for Computational Linguistics*, 2:193–206.

Nathan Schneider, Dirk Hovy, Anders Johannsen, and Marine Carpuat. 2016. SemEval-2016 Task 10: Detecting Minimal Semantic Units and their Meanings (DiMSUM). In *Proc. of SemEval*, pages 546–559, San Diego, California, USA.

Nathan Schneider, Jena D. Hwang, Vivek Srikumar, Jakob Prange, Austin Blodgett, Sarah R. Moeller, Aviram Stern, Adi Bitan, and Omri Abend. 2018. Comprehensive supersense disambiguation of English prepositions and possessives. In *Proc. of ACL*, pages 185–196, Melbourne, Australia.

Nathan Schneider, Behrang Mohit, Chris Dyer, Kemal Oflazer, and Noah A. Smith. 2013. Supersense tagging for Arabic: the MT-in-the-middle attack. In *Proc. of NAACL-HLT*, pages 661–667, Atlanta, Georgia, USA.

Nathan Schneider, Spencer Onuffer, Nora Kazour, Emily Danchik, Michael T. Mordowanec, Henrietta Conrad, and Noah A. Smith. 2014b. Comprehensive annotation of multiword expressions in a social web corpus. In *Proc. of LREC*, pages 455–461, Reykjavík, Iceland.

Nathan Schneider and Noah A. Smith. 2015. A corpus and model integrating multiword expressions and supersenses. In *Proc. of NAACL-HLT*, pages 1537–1547, Denver, Colorado.

Frédérique Segond, Anne Schiller, Gregory Grefenstette, and Jean-Pierre Chanod. 1997. An experiment in semantic tagging using hidden Markov model tagging. In *Automatic Information Extraction and Building of Lexical Semantic Resources for NLP Applications: ACL/EACL-97 Workshop Proceedings*, pages 78–81, Madrid, Spain.

Yutaro Shigeto, Ai Azuma, Sorami Hisamoto, Shuhei Kondo, Tomoya Kouse, Keisuke Sakaguchi, Akifumi Yoshimoto, Frances Yung, and Yuji Matsumoto. 2013. Construction of English MWE dictionary and its application to POS tagging. In *Proc. of the 9th Workshop on Multiword Expressions*, pages 139–144, Atlanta, Georgia, USA.

Vered Shwartz and Ido Dagan. 2019. Still a pain in the neck: Evaluating text representations on lexical composition. *Transactions of the Association for Computational Linguistics*, 7:403–419.

Shiva Taslimipoor, Omid Rohanian, and Le An Ha.
2019. Cross-lingual transfer learning and multitask
learning for capturing multiword expressions. In
Proc. of the Joint Workshop on Multiword Expressions and WordNet (MWE-WN 2019), pages 155–
161, Florence, Italy.

Veronika Vincze, István Nagy T., and Gábor Berend.
2011. Multiword expressions and named entities in
the Wiki50 corpus. In *Proc. of RANLP*, pages 289–
295, Hissar, Bulgaria.

Abigail Walsh, Claire Bonial, Kristina Geeraert, John P.
McCrae, Nathan Schneider, and Clarissa Somers.
2018. Constructing an annotated corpus of verbal
MWEs for English. In *Proc. of LAW-MWE-CxG-2018*, pages 193–200, Santa Fe, New Mexico, USA.

Yilun Zhu, Yang Liu, Siyao Peng, Austin Blodgett,
Yushi Zhao, and Nathan Schneider. 2019. Adpositional Supersenses for Mandarin Chinese. In *Proc.
of SCiL*, volume 2, pages 334–337, New York, NY,
USA.

Finding BERT's Idiomatic Key

Vasudevan Nedumpozhimana and John D. Kelleher
ADAPT Research Center
Technological University Dublin
Dublin, Ireland
{Vasudevan.Nedumpozhimana, john.d.kelleher}@tudublin.ie

Abstract

Sentence embeddings encode information relating to the usage of idioms in a sentence. This paper reports a set of experiments that combine a probing methodology with input masking to analyse where in a sentence this idiomatic information is taken from, and what form it takes. Our results indicate that BERT's idiomatic key is primarily found within an idiomatic expression, but also draws on information from the surrounding context. Also, BERT can distinguish between the disruption in a sentence caused by words missing and the incongruity caused by idiomatic usage.

1 Introduction

Idioms occur in almost all languages, however the processing of idioms by NLP systems remains extremely challenging (Villavicencio et al., 2005; Sporleder and Li, 2009; Salton et al., 2014). One reason for this is that many expressions can be used both literally or idiomatically. Fazly et al. (2009) distinguish between identifying whether an expression has an idiomatic sense (*idiom type* classification) and identifying whether a particular usage of an expression is idiomatic (*idiom token* classification), and focus their work on analysing the canonical form (lexical and syntactic) of idiomatic expressions. The related work on *idiom token* classification at a sentence level includes (Sporleder and Li, 2009; Li and Sporleder, 2010a,b; Peng and Feldman, 2017; Fazly et al., 2009; Salton et al., 2016, 2017). Of particular relevance is Salton et al. (2016) which demonstrated that it is possible to train a generic (as distinct to expression specific) idiom token classifier using distributed sentence embeddings. Of note here is that Salton et al. (2016) used Skip-Thought vectors rather than the more recent contextual embeddings such as BERT (Devlin et al., 2019) and also that these results indicate

that language model based embeddings encode information from a sentence relating to the literal or idiomatic usage of expressions.

Cacciari and Tabossi (1988) proposed one of the most accepted psycholinguistic theories of how humans identify the presence of an idiom. This theory posits that there is a part of every idiomatic expression that must be processed (i.e., accessed from the mental lexicon) before the idiomatic meaning of the expression can be recognised. This special part of an idiomatic expression is known as the *idiomatic key*. The theory leaves open how incongruency between an expression and the context it occurs within might trigger a figurative interpretation.

Given the empirical results of Salton et al. (2016) and the psycholinguistic work of Cacciari and Tabossi (1988) one question that arises is where in a sentence is the *idiomatic key* for models such as BERT: is it predominantly local to the expression or not? Note, that here we are using a broader concept of idiomatic key than that proposed by Cacciari and Tabossi (1988): they limit the idiomatic key to be a part of an expression, whereas we use the concept of idiomatic key to be the part of a sentence that provides BERT with a signal that an expression is being using idiomatically. Answering the question of where BERT's idiomatic key is can provide insight into how BERT, and similar systems work, and also into human language processing. In this paper we address this question by using a probing style experiment (Conneau et al., 2018) combined with various input masking techniques.

Section 2 describes the dataset, embeddings, and model types that we use. Section 3 reports baseline experiments that examine the strength of the idiomatic usage signal encoded in BERT embeddings, and Section 4 reports a second set of experiments where various masking techniques are used to analyse where in a sentence BERT's *idiomatic key* is located. Section 5 sets out our conclusions.

57

Proceedings of the 17th Workshop on Multiword Expressions, pages 57–62
Bangkok, Thailand (online), August 6, 2021. ©2021 Association for Computational Linguistics

2 Data, Embeddings, and Models

A probing experiment tests for the presence of information relating to a linguistic phenomenon within an embedding. The methodology involves using the embedding as the input to a model that is trained to predict whether the linguistic phenomenon is present in the original linguistic input or not. If the model can achieve a high-accuracy on the task this is taken as evidence that the embedding encodes information on the linguistic phenomenon. Indeed, the work by Salton et al. (2016) is an early example of probing, in that instance probing Skip-Thought vectors and idiom token classification.

For our experiments we used the VNIC data set (Cook et al., 2008). The VNIC dataset contains 2984 sentences across 56 idiomatic expressions. Each sentence contains one of the target expressions and is labelled as: idiomatic, literal or unknown usage. Of these 2984 sentences 2016 sentences are used in idiomatic sense, 550 sentences are used in literal sense, and remaining sentences are labelled as unknown. A model trained on such an imbalanced dataset will likely be biased towards the majority class label (in this case the idiomatic label) and such a bias would be a confounding factor in our masking experiments. In our experimental setup the signal we use to identify BERT's idiomatic key is how the ablation of different types of information (via various forms of masking) affects the likelihood BERT returns for idiomatic usage within a sentence. If BERT is biased towards idiomatic usage based on class distribution untangling the effects of this bias from the effects of information ablation would make our analysis much more complex. To control for this bias we downsampled the dataset to make sure that the dataset has a balanced label distribution. We selected all 550 sentences with literal usage and 550 sentences with idiomatic usage by randomly down sampling 2016 idiomatic sentences for our probing experiment. We repeated the down sampling of idiomatic sentences 20 times to prepare 20 different versions of the dataset, and for each version of the down sampled dataset we then split the 1100 sentences into a training set with 80% of samples and a testing set with the remaining 20% of samples with stratified label distribution. Consequently, downsampling not only enables us to balance the class labels but also gives this opportunity to repeat experiment with many versions of dataset and this provides the benefit of cross validation. For each experiment we have run the experiment independently on each of the 20 down sampled versions of the dataset, and then calculated the macro average score across these 20 independent runs.

For each down sampled version of the dataset we used a bert-base-uncased pretrained BERT model[1] to generate sentence embeddings (Devlin et al., 2019). We use this version of BERT as a representative of BERT based (transformer based) language model family. In this experiment our focus is to analyse the pretained BERT model, and the information signals it uses for the task of idiom token identification, rather than to extend the current state of the art performance on this task and therefore we didn't fine tune the BERT model. This BERT model gives 12 layers of 768 dimensional embeddings for each word in a sentence. We used the average of the final layer of word embeddings as the sentence embedding.

For our probing experiments we trained a multi-layer perceptron (MLP) on the training split of each dataset to predict a high probability for embeddings of idiomatic usage sentences and low probability for embeddings of literal usage sentences. The MLP with 768 inputs, one hidden layer of 100 ReLUs, and a logistic unit output layer was implemented using Scikit-learn library (Pedregosa et al., 2011). The MLP was trained using an Adam solver (Kingma and Ba, 2014) using the Scikit-learn default hyper parameters and a convergence criterion of 200 epochs. We define the probability score of a sentence predicted by the trained MLP model as the score of idiomaticity of that sentence.

3 Baseline Results

To evaluate the MLP we use the mean idiomaticity scores on the idiomatic and literal segments of the test sets, where the ideal score of an idiomatic sentence is 1.00 and a literal sentence is 0.00. Consequently, the closer the average score returned by the model on idiomatic sentences is to 1.00 the stronger the model, and similarly the closer the average score returned by the model on literal sentences is to 0.00 the stronger the model. The *Baseline* scores in Table 1 show the average scores returned by the models on the idiomatic and literal segments of the test sets. The MLPs have good performance on both idiomatic sentences (0.85 against the ideal 1.00) and on literal sentences (0.17 against

---

[1] 12-layer, 768-hidden, 12-heads, and 110M parameters, trained on lower-cased English text

the ideal 0.00). This strong performance indicates that the MLPs effectively predict the idiomaticity of both idiomatic and literal sentences, and furthermore that BERT sentence embeddings encode information relating to idiomatic usage.

4 Masking Experiments

Our primary objective is to locate where BERT's idiomatic key is located within a sentence, is it concentrated within the expression or not. In order to gather information on this we conducted an experiment to test how the idiomaticity scores returned by the MLP model changed when we masked different parts of the input. The intuition behind our experimental design is that if we mask the components of a sentence that are informative regarding idiomatic usage within the sentence this should result in the MLP model shifting their scores for a sentence towards 0.5 in an amount that is proportional to the informativeness of the masked component, because the model will have less certainty regarding the idiomatic, or literal, usage within the sentence. Note, that the test sets used in these masking experiments are the same 20 test sets that were used in the baseline experiments. Furthermore, the MLP model tested on each test set is the same model trained using the corresponding training split for the baseline experiment (i.e., the training set is not masked). Consequently, the baseline results discussed above are for the same models used in this experiment.

For this experiment a natural part of a sentence to mask is the expression whose idiomatic usage within the sentence is being assessed. However, given that the idiomatic key may be located outside the target expression we also need to select other components of sentences to be masked. There are many ways we could have selected these components. However, all the target expressions in our data contain two words, a verb and a noun, and so for each sentence we randomly selected two other words for masking. This method has the advantages of simplicity and also matching the number of words masked in the sentence when masking an expression or masking outside the expression.

As a measure for the informativeness of a component (target expression or random selection) with respect to idiomatic usage within the sentence we define *differential idiomaticity* as the difference in idiomaticity score returned by the MLP model for the sentence embedding when the component is present in the input and when it is masked. Our

models are trained to score idiomatic usage sentences close to 1.00 and so we expect that for idiomatic usage sentences differential idiomaticity will be positive (between 0.00 and 1.00) because masking part of the input will likely shift the model score towards 0 and the difference between the score for the unmasked input and the masked input will then be positive. Conversely, for literal sentences we expect that differential idiomaticity will be a negative (between 0.00 and -1.00). Overall, the informativeness of a component with respect to idiomatic usage in a sentence is captured by the magnitude of its differential idiomaticity.

We followed two strategies for masking information in a sentence: *word masking* and *embedding masking*. In the word masking strategy, we replace the words in a sentence to be masked using the same [MASK] token as that used by Devlin et al. (2019). Our word masking strategy completely blocks the information from masked words. However, the resulting sentence may not be a valid sentence. Consequently, we also tested a second masking strategy that retained the words in the sentence input into BERT but masked the word embeddings prior to calculating the sentence embedding. We generate the sentence embeddings by taking the average of the final layer of BERT embeddings of all words in the sentence. However, when we apply embedding masking we don't include the final layer embeddings of the words to be masked in the calculation of the sentence embedding.

5 Results and Conclusions

Table 1 presents the average idiomaticity and the differential idiomaticity with respect to Baseline along with p-values from the experiment broken down by component being masked (target expression or random words) and the type of sentence (idiomatic or literal usage) by using the trained MLP model. As noted in the preceding section, we consider the absolute value of differential idiomaticity as an indication of idiomatic information in a component.

For idiomatic sentences we observe that using a word masking strategy masking either the target expression or random words outside of the expression resulted in a statistically significant difference in idiomaticity scores compared with the baseline results (the differential idiomaticity of 0.02 for random word masking has a p-value of 0.026 and the differential idiomaticity of 0.06 for masking the

Masking	Idiomatic			Literal		
	Id	DId	p-value	Id	DId	p-value
Baseline	0.85	-	-	0.17	-	-
Target Expn + Word Mask	0.79	0.06	1.12E-05	0.24	-0.08	2.83E-07
Target Expn + Emb Mask	0.83	0.02	1.91E-11	0.19	-0.02	4.07E-16
Rand Word + Word Mask	0.83	0.02	0.026	0.17	0.00	0.854
Rand Word + Emb Mask	0.85	0.00	0.313	0.17	0.00	0.378

Table 1: Mean Idiomaticities (Id) and Mean Differential Idiomaticities (DId) and p-values

target expression has a p-value of $1.12E-05$). The fact that masking the words in the target expression has a larger effect on idiomaticity compared with masking random words outside the expression indicates that the idiomatic key is primarily concentrated within the target expressions, which makes intuitive sense. However, the fact that the differential idiomaticity for random word masking is also statistically significant indicates that for BERT the idiomatic key is not restricted to be within the target expression, but may also occur in in the context. Finally, the fact that word masking has a larger impact on idiomaticity compared with embedding masking suggests that the idiomatic key is not equivalent to a disruption of any type in the sentence, we will return to this below.

For literal sentences, masking of target expression resulted in a statistically significant difference in idiomaticity (the mean differential idiomaticity of -0.08 with word masking has a p-value of $2.83E-07$ and the mean differential idiomaticity of -0.02 with embedding masking has a p-value of $4.07E-16$), but masking of random words outside target expression shows insignificant difference with both word masking and embedding masking approaches (negligibly small mean differential idiomaticity with word and embedding masking having p-values 0.854 and 0.378 respectively). These results generally mirror the results on idiomatic sentences and suggest that the signal BERT uses to distinguish literal from idiomatic usages of an expression is primarily found in the expression itself.

One question that arises is whether these differential idiomaticity scores actually relate to the removal of specific information relating to idiomatic usage from an embedding or just reflect disruption within the sentence. The signal encoded in an embedding for idiomatic usage within a sentence may, in fact, be some form of high-perplexity or incongruity in the sentence, and so it is very difficult to disentangle different forms of disruption within a

sentence: how should we disentangle the surprise of an unexpected word from the surprise of a missing word? Indeed, it may be that by introducing some particular form of disruption (via masking) into a BERT sentence embedding we are in fact simulating an idiomatic key.

The differential idiomaticity scores for the embedding masking is a potential source of information relevant to this topic. The fact that the differential idiomaticity scores resulting from embedding masking are smaller than those generated by word masking reflects the fact that the self-attention mechanism within the BERT architecture means that the final layer embedding for a word encodes information from other words in the sentence. Consequently, the final sentence embedding generated under embedding masking indirectly encodes the information from the masked embeddings (because the unmasked embeddings that are included encode information about the words corresponding to the masked embeddings) and as a result the sentence embedding is less disrupted by the masking process. In other words, the missing word effect is not as strong under embedding masking but the word incongruity effects caused by idiomatic usage could still be present. Given this, the weak differential idiomaticity scores generated using embedding masking might indicate that BERT is able to encode word incongruity within a sentence embedding even if the embedding for the word itself is not included in final calculation of the sentence embedding, and consequently the idiom token classifiers are still able to confidently predict idiomatic usage. More generally, it suggest that BERT embeddings distinguish between the disruption caused by missing words and the type of incongruity introduced into a sentence by the idiomatic usage of an expression.

Another factor to consider here is that in our dataset the target expressions are verb noun compounds. Consequently, these expressions are made up of content words that likely contain topical information. Our experiment shows significant differences in idiomaticity on both idiomatic and literal sentences after masking the target expression. The rise in idiomaticity in literal sentences due to target expression masking might be because of the incongruity caused by the absence of content words in the target expression. Similarly the reduction of idiomaticity in idiomatic sentences after the target expression masking might be because of the reduced incongruity within the sentence caused by the absence of an idiomatic target expression. This suggests that the incongruity caused by presence or absence of a target expression, or other content words, which have topical information might be the idiomatic key of BERT and further experiments are needed to investigate this.

In conclusion, our results indicate that BERT's idiomatic key is primarily found within an idiomatic expression itself, but also relies on some information from the surrounding context. Also, BERT can distinguish between the disruption in a sentence caused by words missing and the incongruity introduced by idiomatic usage. Further investigation regarding the idiomatic information in the surrounding context (for example, by masking different categories of words, such as content words, topical key words, or words with different part of speech categorization) is proposed for future research.

Acknowledgments

This work was partly supported by the ADAPT Centre which is funded under the SFI Research Centres Programme (Grant 13/RC/2106_P2) and is co-funded under the European Regional Development Funds.

References

Cristina Cacciari and Patrizia Tabossi. 1988. The comprehension of idioms. *Journal of Memory and Language*, 27:668–683.

Alexis Conneau, German Kruszewski, Guillaume Lample, Loïc Barrault, and Marco Baroni. 2018. What you can cram into a single $&!#* vector: Probing sentence embeddings for linguistic properties. In *Proceedings of the 56th Annual Meeting of the Association for Computational Linguistics (Volume 1: Long Papers)*, pages 2126–2136, Melbourne, Australia. Association for Computational Linguistics.

Paul Cook, Afsaneh Fazly, and Suzanne Stevenson. 2008. The VNC-tokens dataset. In *Proceedings of the LREC Workshop Towards a Shared Task for Multiword Expressions (MWE 2008)*, pages 19–22.

Jacob Devlin, Ming-Wei Chang, Kenton Lee, and Kristina Toutanova. 2019. BERT: Pre-training of deep bidirectional transformers for language understanding. In *Proceedings of the 2019 Conference of the North American Chapter of the Association for Computational Linguistics: Human Language Technologies, Volume 1 (Long and Short Papers)*, pages 4171–4186, Minneapolis, Minnesota. Association for Computational Linguistics.

Afsaneh Fazly, Paul Cook, and Suzanne Stevenson. 2009. Unsupervised type and token identification of idiomatic expressions. *Comput. Linguist.*, 35(1):61–103.

Diederik P. Kingma and Jimmy Ba. 2014. Adam: A method for stochastic optimization. Cite arxiv:1412.6980Comment: Published as a conference paper at the 3rd International Conference for Learning Representations, San Diego, 2015.

Linlin Li and Caroline Sporleder. 2010a. Linguistic cues for distinguishing literal and non-literal usages. In *Proceedings of the 23rd International Conference on Computational Linguistics: Posters*, COLING '10, pages 683–691, Stroudsburg, PA, USA. Association for Computational Linguistics.

Linlin Li and Caroline Sporleder. 2010b. Using Gaussian mixture models to detect figurative language in context. In *Human Language Technologies: The 2010 Annual Conference of the North American Chapter of the Association for Computational Linguistics*, pages 297–300, Los Angeles, California. Association for Computational Linguistics.

Fabian Pedregosa, Gaël Varoquaux, Alexandre Gramfort, Vincent Michel, Bertrand Thirion, Olivier Grisel, Mathieu Blondel, Peter Prettenhofer, Ron Weiss, Vincent Dubourg, et al. 2011. Scikit-learn: Machine learning in python. *Journal of machine learning research*, 12(Oct):2825–2830.

Jing Peng and Anna Feldman. 2017. Automatic idiom recognition with word embeddings. In *Information Management and Big Data - 2nd Annual International Symposium, SIMBig 2015 and 3rd Annual International Symposium, SIMBig 2016, Revised Selected Papers*, Communications in Computer and Information Science, pages 17–29. Springer Verlag.

Giancarlo Salton, Robert Ross, and John Kelleher. 2014. An empirical study of the impact of idioms on phrase based statistical machine translation of English to Brazilian-Portuguese. In *Proceedings of the 3rd Workshop on Hybrid Approaches to Machine Translation (HyTra)*, pages 36–41, Gothenburg, Sweden. Association for Computational Linguistics.

Giancarlo Salton, Robert Ross, and John Kelleher. 2016. Idiom token classification using sentential distributed semantics. In *Proceedings of the 54th Annual Meeting of the Association for Computational Linguistics (Volume 1: Long Papers)*, pages 194–204, Berlin, Germany. Association for Computational Linguistics.

Giancarlo Salton, Robert Ross, and John Kelleher. 2017. Idiom type identification with smoothed lexical features and a maximum margin classifier. In *Proceedings of the International Conference Recent Advances in Natural Language Processing, RANLP 2017*, pages 642–651, Varna, Bulgaria. INCOMA Ltd.

Caroline Sporleder and Linlin Li. 2009. Unsupervised recognition of literal and non-literal use of idiomatic expressions. In *Proceedings of the 12th Conference of the European Chapter of the Association for Computational Linguistics*, EACL '09, pages 754–762, Stroudsburg, PA, USA. Association for Computational Linguistics.

Aline Villavicencio, Francis Bond, Anna Korhonen, and Diana McCarthy. 2005. Editorial: Introduction to the special issue on multiword expressions: Having a crack at a hard nut. *Comput. Speech Lang.*, 19(4):365–377.

Light Verb Constructions and Their Families – A Corpus Study on German *stehen unter*-LVCs

Jens Fleischhauer

Department of General Linguistics
Heinrich Heine Universität Düsseldorf
Universitätsstraße 1, 40225 Düsseldorf, Germany
`fleischhauer@phil.uni-duesseldorf.de`

Abstract

The paper reports on a corpus study of German light verb constructions (LVCs). LVCs come in families which exemplify systematic interpretation patterns. The paper's aim is to account for the properties determining these patterns on the basis of a corpus study on German LVCs of the type '*stehen unter* NP' ('stand under NP').

1   Introduction: LVCs and their families

Light verb constructions (LVC) are a specific type of predicatively used multiword expressions.[1] A LVC consists of a semantically light verb and a phrasal element, e.g., a PP as in the German examples in (1).

(1)   a.   *unter Beobachtung stehen*
             'be under observation' (lit. under observation stand)
       b.   *unter Schutz stehen*
             'be under protection' (lit. under protection stand)

The German LVCs in (1) consist of the light verb *stehen* 'stand' and a prepositional phrase (PP) headed by *unter* 'under'. *Stehen* is, according to Kamber (2008), one of the most frequently occurring light verbs in German.

The English notion 'light verb' goes back to Jespersen (1942) who assumed that light verb are semantically empty. This position has been questioned by a number of authors (e.g. Isoda 1991; Brugman 2001; Butt 1995; Butt and Geuder 2001, 2003; Butt and Lahiri 2013; Fleischhauer and Neisani 2020) who insist that the light verb makes at least a subtle contribution to the LVC's overall meaning. This position also prevails in the

German research tradition. von Polenz (1963) – who introduced the corresponding German notion 'Funktionsverb' (lit. function verb)– recognized that light verbs contribute in terms of aktionsart features as well as causativity. Thus, the light verb is not semantically empty but only semantically reduced compared to its corresponding heavy uses.

In its heavy use (2-a) *stehen* expresses that its subject referent is spatially located in an upright posture; the spatial location is specified by the PP-complement (see Gamerschlag et al. 2013 for a detailed discussion of German posture verbs). As a light verb, *stehen* does not express that its subject referent is being spatially located (2-b). Rather, the verb only contributes to the complex predicate's event structure. LVCs headed by *stehen* always express state predications (e.g. von Polenz, 1963, 1987; Fleischhauer and Gamerschlag, 2019; Fleischhauer et al., 2019).

(2)   a.   *Der Mann steht   unter dem Dach.*
             the man   stands under the roof
             'The man is standing under the roof.'
       b.   *Der Mann steht   unter Schock.*
             the man   stands under shock
             'The man is shocked/stressed.'

The PP-internal noun provides the LVC's main predicational content. The LVC in (2-b) expresses that the subject referent is in a state of shock; substituting the noun by e.g. *Stress* 'stress' results in a different predication. The LVC *unter Stress stehen* 'be stressed' (lit. under stress stand) expresses that the subject referent is in a state of stress.

Like simplex predicates, LVCs can be classified with respect to semantic features like aktionsart and causativity. These features have been systematically related to the light verb's lexical meaning (e.g. von Polenz 1963, 1987). But is has rarely been noticed that systematicity is also found on a semantically deeper level. The LVCs in (1) exem-

---

[1] The research reported in this paper is part of the project 'Funktionsverbgefüge: Familien & Komposition' founded by the German Research Foundation (HE 8721/1-1).

Proceedings of the 17th Workshop on Multiword Expressions, pages 63–69
Bangkok, Thailand (online), August 6, 2021. ©2021 Association for Computational Linguistics

plify a different interpretation pattern from those in (2). Following Nunberg et al. (1994), I use the label 'family' to designate LVCs which conform to the same interpretation pattern. The notion of a LVC-family is defined as follows (following Fleischhauer 2019, 32, Fleischhauer and Turus in press):

(3)   Light verb constructions form a family if (i) they only show variance with respect to their NP element, and (ii) they exemplify the same interpretational pattern.

The LVCs in (1) belong to a family I call 'event passive-family' since they are paraphrased by an event passive construction (so-called *werden* 'become'-passive). *Unter Beobachtung stehen* in (1-a) is paraphrased as 'beobachtet werden' ('be observed' lit. observed become). The two LVCs *unter Schock stehen* 'be shocked' (2-b) and *unter Stress stehen* 'be stressed' superficially look like the LVCs in (1) but resist an event passive paraphrase. Instead, they are paraphrased by a state passive construction (*sein* 'be' + passive participle).[2] *Unter Schock stehen* (2-b), for example, is paraphrased as 'geschockt sein' ('be shocked'; lit. shocked be).

The current paper presents a first systematic case study of LVC-families. The central questions are: Which LVCs are members of these families? And, what are the characteristic properties of the members of the individual families? These questions have been explored on the basis of a corpus study.

2   Corpus study

For the corpus study on German *stehen unter*-LVCs, I used the Tagged-C2 archive of the German reference corpus (DeReKo). The archive basically contains newspaper articles and consists of 1.022.895.699 words organized in 4.491.138 texts. The corpus search has been carried out using the search engine COSMAS II.

I will start a brief discussion of the search criterion used for the corpus study and then proceed by discussing the individual annotation steps. The annotation has been independently done by two annotators, in case of disagreement a third annotator has been consulted.

---

[2]For a discussion of formal as well as semantic differences of the two mentioned German passive constructions, see Maienborn (2007).

2.1   Search criterion

LVCs cannot directly be identified within the German reference corpus. The reasons for this are twofold. First, LVCs cannot be distinguished from regular predicate-argument constructions on the basis of morphosyntactic criteria. The two sentences in (2) look superficially similar even though the second one contains a LVC. Some authors propose that LVCs can be distinguished from regular predicate-argument constructions on the basis of the semantic type of the PP-internal noun. LVCs require an eventive noun in PP-internal position, whereas regular predicate-argument constructions do not (e.g. von Polenz, 1963, 1987; Engelen, 1968; Persson, 1994; Helbig, 1984, 2006; Langer, 2004, 2005; Ježek, 2016; Savary et al., 2018). This criterion is refuted by some authors like, for example, Klein (1968); Herrlitz (1973); Schwall (1991); Rostila (2001); Hanks et al. (2006). In addition, the language data discussed in section 3 indicate that LVCs are not restricted to eventive nouns in PP-internal position but license, for example, artefact nouns as well.

Second, the individual components of a LVC can be separated by lexical material which does not belong to the MWE. In the interrogative sentence in (4), the subject NP intervenes between the light verb and the *unter*-PP. Nagy T. et al. (2020, 326) mention that a discontinuous realization of LVCs is particularly frequent in German (compared to e.g. English, Spanish and Hungarian); this is probably due to general constraints on German word order. Discontinuity is a challenging property for the identification of MWEs in general (e.g. Constant et al., 2017).

(4)   *Steht der Verdächtige unter Beobachtung?*
        'Is the suspect under observation?'

Given the mentioned difficulties in identifying LVCs, I searched for all occurrences of inflected *stehen* and the preposition *unter* realized within the same sentence (search string '&stehen \s0 unter'). This search criterion yielded 80255 hits of which 8023 sentences (approx. 10% of all hits) have been randomly collected for manual annotation. 55 sentences have been excluded from the annotation procedure since they were incomplete.

Although there exists substantive literature on the annotation of MWEs in general and of LVCs in particular (e.g. Krenn 2008; Tu and Roth 2011; Rácz et al. 2014; Savary et al. 2018; Nagy T. et al. 2020), these studies differ in scope from the present one. The present study is not concerned with LVCs in general or LVCs headed by a specific type of light verb but is directed at a specific combination of light verb and preposition. This allowed using more specific annotation criteria which were directly tailored for this type of construction.

LVC-families have not been the subject of corpus studies so far.

2.2 First annotation step

The *unter*-PP is a syntactic complement of *stehen*, both in the verb's light as well as heavy uses. In a first annotation step, we singled out those sentences in which the *unter*-PP is not realized as the verb's complement. The relevant test criterion is whether the PP can be left out without affecting the acceptability of the resulting sentence. If not, the PP is classified as being a complement of *stehen*. The results of the first annotation step are summarized in Table 1.

PP complement	PP not complement
5822	2146

Table 1: Results of the first annotation step.

The sentences in which the PP is not a complement of *stehen* were excluded from further analysis.

2.3 Second annotation step

The second annotation step consisted in distinguishing heavy from non-heavy uses of *stehen*. Non-heavy uses comprise light uses as well as what Fazly and Stevenson (2007, 10) term 'abstract uses'. As a heavy verb *stehen* can be substituted by other posture verbs (e.g. *sitzen* 'sit' or *liegen* 'lie') or by purely locational predicates like *positioniert sein* 'be positioned' or *lokalisiert sein* 'be localized'. In (5-a), *stehen* can be substituted by, for example *sitzen* or *liegen* and therefore is classified as a 'heavy' verb.

The substitution of *stehen* by a different posture verb is unacceptable in (5-b). Accordingly, this use of *stehen* is classified as 'non-heavy'.

(5)   a.   *Der Mann steht/liegt/sitzt unter dem*
the man stands/lies/sits under the
Dach.
roof
'The man is standing/sitting/lying under the roof.'

        b.   *Der Mann steht/*liegt/*sitzt unter*
the man stands/sits/lies under
Schock.
shock
'The man is in a state of shock/is shocked.'

The results of the second annotation step are summarized in Table 2. There is a clear preference for *stehen* in combination with the preposition *unter* to be used as a non-heavy verb.

heavy use	non-heavy use
562	5260

Table 2: Results of the second annotation step.

The third annotation step has only been done with respect to the sentences classified as containing a non-heavy use of *stehen*.

2.4 Third annotation step

The final annotation step consisted in identifying LVC-families. Since the focus is on the two LVC-families introduced above, it was only checked whether the combination of light *stehen* and its PP-complement is paraphrased by using a sentence containing an event passive or state passive construction. The two types of paraphrases have already been introduced in Section 1. As summarized in Table 3, 1335 occurrences require an event passive paraphrase and 1524 sentences are paraphrased by use of a state passive construction. The two LVC-families represent 49.23% of all non-heavy uses of *stehen* within the analyzed sample.

event-passive paraphrase	state-passive para-phrase
1335	1524

Table 3: Results of the third annotation step.

An example of a non-heavy use of *stehen* rejecting an event passive or state passive paraphrase is shown in (6). The construction *unter dem Motto stehen* (lit. under the motto stand) is paraphrased as 'have as its motto' which is not a passive paraphrase but a paraphrase expressing abstract (predicative) possession.

Based on the data of the third annotation step, the individual members of the two LVC-families have been identified. The event passive-family is represented by 33 different LVCs; for the the state passive-family 19 different members have been found. The full list of nouns occurring PP-internally in the two families is given in the appendix. With respect to the third annotation step, the two annotators have been in total agreement.

(6) *Das Kinderturnen stand unter dem*
   the children.gymnastic stands under the
   Motto "Max und Moritz".
   motto Max and Moritz
   'The children's gymnastics has as its motto 'Max and Moritz'.' (A98/JAN.01801 St. Galler Tagblatt, 12.01.1998, Ressort: RT-ORT (Abk.); Dorffeststimmung auf die Bühne gezaubert)

3 The semantic type of the PP-internal nouns

In a final step, all nouns occurring PP-internally were classified with respect to the type of object they are denoting. It was first checked whether the PP-internal nouns denote an eventuality. The notion 'eventuality' is used as a cover term for states and events (Bach, 1986). Eventuality-denoting nouns accept temporal (e.g. *gestern* 'yesterday') and aspectual modifiers (e.g. *andauernd* 'continuous') (Fábregas and Marín, 2012; Fleischhauer and Neisani, 2020). Only five nouns (7-a) – all belonging to the state passive-family – reject temporal/aspectual modification. An example of a LVC containing the artefact noun *Drogen* 'drugs' is shown in (7-b). The example expresses that the subject referent is in a state induced by drugs (i.e. is influenced by drugs).

(7) a. *Alkohol* 'alcohol', *Beruhigungsmittel* 'sedative', *Drogen* 'drugs', *Medikamente* 'medicine', *Suchtmittel* 'addictive substances'
  b. *Der Fahrer stand unter Drogen.*
    the driver stood under drugs
    'The driver was under the influence of drugs.'

With respect to the eventuality-denoting nouns, the two LVC-families show clear differences. The PP-internal nouns occurring in the event-passive family denote events, those occurring in the state-passive family are state-denoting. There exist a number of criteria which allow distinguishing event-denoting nouns from state-denoting ones (cf. Fábregas and Marín 2012; Fábregas et al. 2012). Only event-

denoting nouns can be realized as the subject of predicates like *geschehen/passieren* 'happen', *beenden* 'stop/finish' and *unterbrochen sein* 'be interrupted'. For details concerning the criteria, the reader is referred to the mentioned literature.

In Section 1, I introduced the LVC *unter Beobachtung stehen* 'be under observation' as a representative member of the event passive-family. The example in (8) demonstrates that the noun *Beobachtung* 'observation' can be realized as the subject of *geschehen* 'happen'. The noun is also licensed as the subject argument of the other mentioned predicates (not illustrated for reasons of space) and qualifies as being event-denoting.

(8) *Vermutlich geschah die Beobachtung [...]*
   probably happened the observation
   mit Hilfe eines nicht allzu schlechtes
   with help a not all.too bay
   Fernrohrs [...]
   telescope
   'Probably, the observation happened with the help of a not too bad telescope" (http://www.vm2000.net/category/ausgabe-80/; 28.04.2021)

The noun *Schock* 'shock' which occurs in the LVC *unter Schock stehen* 'be shocked' – a representative member of the state passive-family – shows a somewhat more variable behavior. Although *Schock* can be realized as the subject of *geschehen*, as shown in (9), it can neither be realized as the subject argument of *beenden* 'stop/finish' nor of *unterbrochen sein* 'be interrupted'. The cumulative evidence speaks in favor of classifying *Schock* as a state-denoting noun.

(9) *Der erste schwere Schock geschah*
   the first heavy shock happened
   sofort am ersten Abend [...].
   immediately at the first eventing
   'The first heavy shock happened immediately at the first evening [...]'
   (https://www.astrotreff.de/forum/index.php?-thread/172584-out-of-stellaland-oder-das-raunen-der-kleinodien/; 01.06.2021)

The interpretational difference observed between the LVCs of the two families is not arbitrary but results form the specific meaning of the nouns licensed in PP-internal position. Event-denoting nouns allow for an event-passive interpretation, state nouns result in a state passive reading. The artefact nouns *Alkohol* 'alcohol', *Drogen* 'drugs', *Suchtmittel* 'addictive substances', *Beruhigungsmittel* 'sedative' and *Medikamente* 'medicine' are associated with a specific state – the state of being intoxicated by the respective substance – and give rise for a state passive reading as well. This interpretation is not restricted to the use of these nouns within the mentioned LVC since it is also found without the light verb. The nouns *Drogen* 'drugs' and *Alkohol* 'alcohol' are conjoined with a PP headed by *unter* in (10) which is realized as an adjunct PP. Like in (7-b), the PP indicates that the subject referent has been under the influence of drugs and alcohol.

(10) *25-Jähriger fährt unter Drogen und*
   25-year_old drives under drugs and
   Alkohol
   alcohol
   '25-year-old is driving under (the influence of) drugs and alcohol'
   (BRZ08/JUL.09227 Braunschweiger Zeitung, 17.07.2008; 25-Jähriger fährt unter Drogen und Alkohol)

Not only *Drogen* can be realized within an *unter*-PP without light *stehen*; the same is true of the other nouns occurring in the two families. This is a relevant observation as it demonstrated that the passive-like interpretation is only dependent on this specific use of the preposition *unter*[3] but neither on the light verb nor on the light verb construction as such. The basic function of the light verb is embedding the passive-like meaning expressed by the PP within a state predication.

4 Conclusion & Outlook

The paper started from the observation that LVCs instantiated by the same morphosyntactic type – in our case '*stehen + unter*' – are heterogeneous with respect to their interpretation. LVCs of this type exemplify (at least) two different systematic interpretation patterns (which have been termed 'families'). Both families share a passive-like interpretation which has been related to the specific use of the preposition *unter*. The differences between the two families have been related to the semantic type of the PP-internal nouns. The existence of LVC-families has (to the best of my knowledge) so far only been recognized for Persian LVCs (e.g.

Family, 2006, 2008, 2011, 2014) but it has been gone unnoticed for other languages (especially for German). It will be definitely worth investigating whether we come across similar or even the same LVC-families in other languages. A natural candidate to look at might be Dutch which – in difference to other languages as for example Turkish or Persian – shows a light use of a verb meaning 'stand'.

Another question to be investigated in the future is whether we can identify further characteristics with respect to which the mentioned LVC-families differ from each other. A promising feature to look at is causativization since it seems to be the case that the two families show different preferences in the choice of their causative light verb. LVCs of the event passive-family prefer *stehen* 'put' (lit. cause to stand), those of the state passive-family prefer *setzen* 'put' (lit. cause to sit). The results of a limited corpus study on the distribution of the two causative LVCs *stellen* and *setzen* are summarized in Table 4. The first two LVCs belong to the event passive-family, the second two LVCs are of the state passive-family. Each LVC has been individually searched for within the German reference corpus (search strings: '&stellen \s0 unter N' and '&setzen \s0 unter N'; 'N' has been replaced by the individual nouns.

	stellen	*setzen*
unter Beobachtung 'under observation'	201	4
unter Schutz 'under protection'	2179	0
unter Schock 'under shock'	1	7
unter Stress 'under stress'	1	244

Table 4: Preferences in the choice of causative light verbs.

Due to reasons of space, I cannot go into further details (especially with respect to the motivation of the different preferences) but take this as a promising starting point for a continuation study on the different families of *stehen unter*-LVCs.

Concerning further automation, we are planing to train learning algorithms on the basis of the annotated data set for the automatic identification of *stehen*-LVCs.

---

[3]For an overview on different meanings realized by *unter*, see Kiss et al. (2016).

References

Emmon Bach. 1986. The Algebra of Events. *Linguistics and Philosophy*, 9:5–16.

Claudia Brugman. 2001. Light verbs and polysemy. *Language Sciences*, 23(4/5):551–578.

Miriam Butt. 1995. *The structure of complex predicates*. CSLI Publications, Stanford.

Miriam Butt and Wilhelm Geuder. 2001. On the (Semi)Lexical Status of Light Verbs. In Norbert Corver and Henk van Riemsdijk, editors, *Semilexical Categories: On the content of function words and the function of content words*, pages 323–370. Mouton, Berlin.

Miriam Butt and Wilhelm Geuder. 2003. Light verbs in Urdu and grammaticalization. In Regine Eckardt, Klaus von Heusinger, and Christoph Schwarze, editors, *Words in Time*, pages 295–350. Mouton de Gruyter, Berlin/ New York.

Miriam Butt and Aditi Lahiri. 2013. Diachronic pertinacity of light verbs. *Lingua*, 135:7–29.

Mathieu Constant, Gülşen Eryiğit, Johanna Montiy, Lonneke van der Plasz, Carlos Ramisch, Michael Rosnerz, and Amalia Todirascuk. 2017. Multiword Expression Processing: A Survey. *Computational Linguistics*, 43(4):837–892.

Leibniz-Institut für Deutsche Sprache. 2020. *COSMAS II (Corpus Search, Management and Analysis System)*. Leibniz-Institut für Deutsche Sprache, Mannheim.

Leibniz-Institut für Deutsche Sprache. 2021. *Deutsches Referenzkorpus / Archiv der Korpora geschriebener Gegenwartssprache 2021-I (Release vom 02.02.2021)*. Leibniz-Institut für Deutsche Sprache, Mannheim.

Bernhard Engelen. 1968. Zum System der Funktionsverbgefüge. *Wirkendes Wort*, 18:289–303.

Antonio Fábregas and Rafael Marín. 2012. The role of Aktionsart in deverbal nouns: State nominalizations across languages. *Journal of Linguistics*, 48:35–70.

Antonio Fábregas, Rafael Marín, and Louise McNally. 2012. From Psych Verbs to Nouns. In Violeta Demonte and Louise McNally, editors, *Telicity, Change, and State*, pages 162–184. Oxford University Press, Oxford.

Neiloufar Family. 2006. *Explorations of Semantic Space: The Case of Light Verb Constructions in Persian*. Ph.D. thesis, Ecole des Hautes Etudes en Science Sociales, Paris.

Neiloufar Family. 2008. A constructionist account of the "light verb" *xordaen* "eat" in Persian. In Martine Vanhove, editor, *From Polysemy to Semantic Change: Towards a typology of lexical semantic associations*, pages 139–161. John Benjamins, Amsterdam/Philadelphia.

Neiloufar Family. 2011. Verbal islands in Persian. *Folia Linguistica*, 45(1):1–30.

Neiloufar Family. 2014. *Semantic Spaces of Persian Light Verbs*. Brill, Leiden.

Afsaneh Fazly and Suzanne Stevenson. 2007. Distinguishing subtypes of multiword expressions using linguistically-motivated statistical measures. In *Proceedings of the Workshop on A Broader Perspective on Multiword Expressions*, pages 9–16, Prague, Czech Republic. Association for Computational Linguistics.

Jens Fleischhauer. 2019. *The distribution of meaning components – The composition of affectedness and light verb constructions*. Habilitation thesis, Heinrich-Heine Universität Düsseldorf.

Jens Fleischhauer and Thomas Gamerschlag. 2019. Deriving the meaning of light verb constructions – A frame account of German *stehen* 'stand'. In *Yearbook of the German Cognitive Linguistics Association, Vol. 7*, pages 137–156, Berlin/Boston. Mouton de Gruyter.

Jens Fleischhauer, Thomas Gamerschlag, Laura Kallmeyer, and Simon Petitjean. 2019. Towards a compositional analysis of German light verb constructions (LVCs) combining Lexicalized Tree Adjoining Grammar (LTAG) with frame semantics. In *Proceedings of the 13th International Conference on Computational Semantics - Long Papers*, pages 79–90, Gothenburg, Sweden. Association for Computational Linguistics.

Jens Fleischhauer and Mozhgan Neisani. 2020. Adverbial and attributive modification of Persian separable light verb constructions. *Journal of Linguistics*, 56:45–85.

Jens Fleischhauer and Dila Turus. in press. Families of light verb constructions in German legal language contexts — A case study on the 'passive'-family of *stehen unter*-light verb constructions. In Daniel Leisser and Luke Green, editors, *Contemporary Approaches to Legal Linguistics*. LIT Verlag, Berlin/Münster.

Thomas Gamerschlag, Wiebke Petersen, and Liane Ströbel. 2013. Sitting, standing, and lying in frames: A frame-based approach to posture verbs. In Guram Bezhanishvili, Sebastian Löbner, Vincenzo Marra, and Frank Richter, editors, *Selected papers of the 9th International Tbilisi Symposium on Logic, Language, and Computation*, pages 73–93. Springer, Berlin.

Patricks Hanks, Anne Urbschat, and Elke Gehweiler. 2006. German Light Verb Constructions in Corpora and Dictionaries. *International Journal of Lexicography*, 19(4):439–457.

Gerhard Helbig. 1984. Probleme der Beschreibung von Funktionsverbgefügen im Deutschen. In Gerhard Helbig, editor, *Studien zur deutschen Syntax, Band*

2, pages 163–188. Verlag Enzyklopädie Leipzig, Leipzig.

Gerhard Helbig. 2006. Funktionsverbgefüge – Kollokationen – Phraseologismen. In Ulrich Breuer and Irma Hyvärinen, editors, *Wörter – Verbindungen*, pages 165–174. Peter Lang, Frankfurt am Main.

Wolfgang Herrlitz. 1973. *Funktionsverbgefüge vom Typ 'in Erfahrung bringen'*. Niemeyer, Tübingen.

Michio Isoda. 1991. The light verb construction in Japanese. In *Papers from the 27th Regional Meeting of the Chicago Linguistics Society*, pages 261–275.

Otto Jespersen. 1942. *A Modern English Grammar on Historical Principles, Part VI, Morphology*. Ejnar Munksgaard, Copenhagen.

Elisabetta Ježek. 2016. *The Lexicon – An Introduction*. Oxford University Press, Oxford.

Alain Kamber. 2008. *Funktionsverbgefüge – empirisch*. Niemeyer, Tübingen.

Tibor Kiss, Antje Müller, Claudia Roch, Tobias Stadtfeld, Alicia Katharina Börner, and Monika Duzy. 2016. *Ein Handbuch für die Bestimmung und Annotation von Präpositionsbedeutungen im Deutschen*, 2. edition. Bochumer Linguistische Arbeitsberichte. Ruhr-Universität Bochum, Bochum.

Wolfgang Klein. 1968. Zur Kategorisierung der Funktionsverben. *Beiträge zur Linguistik und Informationsverarbeitung*, 13:7–37.

Brigitte Krenn. 2008. Description of evaluation resource -- German PP-verb data. In *Proceedings of MWE 2008*, pages 7–10, Marrakech. European Language Resources Association.

Stefan Langer. 2004. A linguistic test battery for support verb constructions. *Lingvisticæ Investigationes*, 27 (2):171–184.

Stefan Langer. 2005. A formal specification of support verb constructions. In Stefan Langer and Daniel Schnorbusch, editors, *Semantik im Lexikon*, pages 179–202. Narr, Tübingen.

Claudia Maienborn. 2007. Das Zustandspassiv: Grammatische Einordnung – Bildungsbeschränkungen – Interpretationsspielraum. *Zeitschrift für Germanistische Linguistik*, 35:83–115.

István Nagy T., Anita Rácz, and Veronika Vincze. 2020. Detecting light verb constructions across languages. *Natural Language Engineering*, 26(3):319–348.

Geoffrey Nunberg, Ivan A. Sag, and Thomas Wasow. 1994. Idioms. *Language*, 70(3):491–538.

Ingemar Persson. 1994. Die Funktion der Präpositionalphrase mit *durch* im Rahmen der kausativen Struktur. *Deutsche Sprache*, 22:331–352.

Anita Rácz, István Nagy T., and Veronika Vincze. 2014. 4FX: Light verb constructions in a multilingual parallel corpus. In *Proceedings of the Ninth International Conference on Language Resources and Evaluation (LREC'14)*, pages 710–715, Reykjavik, Iceland. European Language Resources Association (ELRA).

Jouni Rostila. 2001. In search of invisible prepositions: Connections between Funktionsverbgefüge and aspectual periphrastics. *Studia Slavica Oldenburgensia*, 8:125–166.

Agata Savary, Marie Candito, Verginica Barbu Mititelu, Eduard Bejček, Fabienne Cap, Slavomír Čéplö, Silvio Ricardo Cordeiro, Gülşen Eryiğit, Voula Giouli, Maarten van Gompel, Yaakov HaCohen-Kerner, Jolanta Kovalevskaite, Simon Krek, Chaya Liebeskind, Johanna Monti, Carla Parra Escartín, Lonneke van der Plas, Behrang QasemiZadeh, Carlos Ramisch, Federico Sangati, Ivelina Stoyanova, and Veronika Vincze. 2018. PARSEME multilingual corpus of verbal multiword expressions. In Stella Markantonatou, Carlos Ramisch, Agata Savary, and Veronika Vincze, editors, *Multiword expressions are depth and in lenght*, pages 87–147. Language Science Press, Berlin.

Ulrike Schwall. 1991. *Aspektualität – Eine semantisch-funktionelle Kategorie*. Gunter Narr Verlag, Tübingen.

Yuancheng Tu and Dan Roth. 2011. Learning English light verb constructions: Contextual or statistical. In *Proceedings of the Workshop on Multiword Expressions: from Parsing and Generation to the Real World*, pages 31–39, Portland, Oregon, USA. Association for Computational Linguistics.

Peter von Polenz. 1963. *Funktionsverben im heutigen Deutsch. Sprache in der rationalisierten Welt*. Schwann, Düsseldorf.

Peter von Polenz. 1987. Funktionsverben, Funktionsverbgefüge und Verwandtes. Vorschläge zur satzsemantischen Lexikographie. *Zeitschrift für germanistische Linguistik*, 15:169–189.